To Carol!

Thank You for All the
You Do.

Coach R. Zunick

Good things you do.

www.
Am14ooCoach.com

The Thinking Room

A New System for Success

Coach Ron Tunick

www.inthethinkingroom.com

The Thinking Room
Written by Ron Tunick
Published Fall 2007
ISBN 978-1-4357-0325-4

Tunick, Ron.

      Thinking Room, The: A New System for Success – 1st edition.

1.   Business
2.   Success
3.   Personal Development

When you read this book, you will:

1. Know how to create your own Thinking Room.

2. Be able to turn thinking into understanding.

3. Recognize your own weaknesses in thinking.

4. Discover your personal path to success.

5. Learn how to manage your time with ease.

6. Become a wiser, more creative decision-maker.

7. Engage in an interactive life audit.

8. Participate in Thinking Room exercises.

9. Experience more peaceful relationships.

10. Conquer your personal doubts.

11. Alter the perception others have of you.

12. Become an expert thinker.

Acknowledgements

Writing a book takes a team and a lot of support from your family. I had both. My family is everything to me and it took my son John to get this book written. John never gave up on his dad and, because of that; I never gave up on myself either. My wife Ellen and my three daughters, Julie, Tracy and Robyn gave me the love to keep going. My daughters are always there for me and that is as good as it gets for any father.

Someone very special too, my editor, Emily Valko, gets a million thanks or maybe a billion thanks. My daughter Tracy put in whole lot of work with the editing as well, and I am so grateful for her dedication.

I also want to thank all the people along the way that made this book possible: the people I observed and the people who shrugged at all my goofy ideas.

I have one comment to my readers: Winners never quit. I owe you a thank you for buying and reading this book. Thank you!

Table of Contents

My Story

"If **I** can do it, **you** can do it."

You've probably heard this line countless times from speakers, books and television. It's a bit of a cliché, but it also resonates with truth. I was inspired by the hard work and dedication of the coaches and mentors that shaped my life. In turn, I want to inspire others to succeed on their journeys. If a kid who came from shaky beginnings was able to work his way to the top, then it goes without saying that you, too, can find the same strength and wisdom.

As a young person growing up in an unstable home, we moved around frequently. I didn't have many friends, found it difficult to trust others, and didn't get the best early education. Yet, even as a child I knew I was going to create a better life for myself one day. I knew I had more to offer, and that I could be successful if I had the right tools. I just didn't know where to look for them.

The thing that saved me was playing sports in high school. My coaches took me under their wings and taught me discipline and dedication. I was not allowed to play if I didn't get decent grades. They even taught me how to look someone in the eye and shake hands with confidence; something I never knew how to convey until my mentors showed me.

I went on to play football in community college, began to work in the library there, and developed a serious interest in books. I had three hours a night to just sit and read, exposing myself to a whole new world. I then transferred to Cal State Northridge to study business. At this point, I was truly motivated about learning and succeeding.

Right out of college, I got a great job where I learned how to improve my communication and likeability factor. I wanted to grow my income, so I got my teaching credential and began teaching night classes at Thousand Oaks High School and Cal Lutheran University in addition to my day job.

I also coached athletic teams on a part-time basis. It was one football coaching job that brought me my first golden opportunity. A football player's father offered me a position at his bank for three times my current salary! I was finally able to keep my head above water financially, so I joined North Ranch Country Club. From this vantage point, I could observe my fellow members, successful people ten or fifteen years older. I realized these men and women spoke differently and approached life differently. They dressed impeccably and communicated with strength and confidence. But their most intriguing quality was the way these people handled their success with quiet humility.

This was the perfect time for me to learn how to conduct myself in a thoughtful and professional manner. For the first time in my life, I was exposed to a different kind of thinking. I would sit at lunch and listen to the other tables' conversations. They had thoughtful, careful discourse. Many of these members came from typical backgrounds, and some came from tough upbringings just like I did.

But they all had something in common. Somehow they were able to make the time and take the time to think. Thinking was an integral part of their daily life. Was it a coincidence that they seemed to make better choices? I began to realize that luck played a much smaller role in success than I'd previously thought. It became clear that I could actually learn how to make better choices, and I could see it in my fellow members.

Several years later I entered the bankcard industry. This is where I spent many years learning and growing as a professional until I was ready to start my own successful business, Nations Transaction Services, Inc. We started as a small, local business and have grown to become a multi-million dollar, full-service payment processor.

I attribute my success to my mentors and my inner persistence, but it took years of missteps for me to reach the knowledgeable place I'm writing to you from today. I was a reactionary. I was prideful. I was going too fast. But I ultimately learned to think and research. I learned that it wasn't the rest of the world that needed to change; it was me that needed to change.

So where does right thinking come from? I guarantee that wherever you are in your life and career, you can work smarter, think more clearly, and achieve your goals sooner than expected. You can have an extraordinary life! Join me on a journey of self-discovery and empowerment in The Thinking Room.

Introduction

Welcome to The Thinking Room, and thank you for reading my book and taking an interest in my story. Since you're reading this today, then you're probably someone who's invested in long-term success.

Perhaps you're interested in earning more money and creating a better lifestyle, or maybe you're simply looking to refine your approach to success. Whatever your motivation, you can expect to benefit from the straightforward, no-nonsense wisdom of someone's who has been there, learned the hard way, and came out the other side with some inspired ways to help you achieve your goals.

The information in this book comes from the accumulated knowledge of a "street guy." This is not a textbook or a specialized reference. This information is based on my real world experience. It took me years to make sense of life and business, but ultimately I figured out how to work smart and make a great living.

I wish there had been a book like this when I was young and just beginning my career. I didn't understand why some people were "winners" and others just couldn't succeed. I had limited resources as a kid and little exposure to successful models.

Why did some folks manage to rise above meager beginnings while others never seemed to break the cycle? The answer is surprisingly intuitive, but it took me years of watching and learning to break my own cycles and take control of my success.

This book is not about wishing or hoping. It is about processing your ideas, thinking like a leader, and most importantly, learning *how to think for yourself*. My goal is to give you a wakeup call. I want to give you the wisdom of my journey (mistakes and all) so that you can become your own success story. Learn to think the right way and you will make better choices. Make better choices and you'll see better opportunities. Learn *how* to think and you will gain strength, self-confidence and the ability to lead. If you're ready to take the leadership role in your own life, then you're ready for The Thinking Room.

Chapter 1

Enter the Thinking Room

As a serious sports fan, the Super Bowl might be my favorite holiday. Every Super Bowl reminds me of how athletes are forced to reinvent themselves. The two teams that make it to the Super Bowl have pushed passed their injuries, dripped gallons of sweat and cried hundreds of painful tears to participate in this most exalted event. They epitomize perseverance, which I think is the greatest character trait you can possess.

These teams reinvent themselves each year; starting with a clean slate and working towards the end game. It always starts with spring training, a time for growth and renewal. Reinventing yourself takes some training as well.

But I'm not asking for your blood, sweat and tears. I'm asking for a serious brain workout. Let me explain…

The bankcard industry is the industry I've chosen to succeed with. It gives me the freedom to make the right choices for my family and for myself. It provides me the standard of living I've come to enjoy: a safe neighborhood, a nice car, and the little things that make me comfortable. All things considered, it's a great life. Perhaps you feel the same about your life. Or perhaps this is the life you're seeking.

But even the successful can become too comfortable. Ask yourself, *Could I improve my business? Could I make more money so I could do more for my family? Could I someday arrive at my own personal Super Bowl?* The answer is yes, yes and yes. It's time to begin to reinvent yourself.

For me, the Super Bowl of business means having no financial worries for my family or myself for the years ahead. It means having the respect of my business peers, and it means enjoying the many fruits of my labor. It means rewarding the team that helped me succeed. And just like star athletes, it means I must continually reinvent myself.

Where do I start? I start in The Thinking Room. For me, The Thinking Room is my office chair. But I'm not facing my computer or paperwork. I face away from my workspace and prop my feet on a footstool. This is where I think. Maybe for you it's a literal room designed to offer a peaceful environment and mental stimulation. Or maybe it's the shower, the treadmill, the sauna, the car, the park bench or the coffee shop.

The Thinking Room is the place where you do your best thinking. But it's also much more than that. In the following chapters, I will explain how The Thinking Room concept revolutionizes your very approach to life and business. Our thoughts are the most powerful tool we have to succeed. Critical thinking has never been more important. We're faced with increased competition, more government regulations, and smarter, better-informed customers.

Mahatma Gandhi said, "Those who know how to think need no teachers." Although I think you always can learn from teachers, this point is well taken. If you learn *how* to think, you'll be your own best teacher. Most likely, you'll end up teaching your peers and colleagues.

So, what do I think about in The Thinking Room?

I think about the leaders in my industry. What are they doing to get to the top? I review the things that I'm doing differently, and consider how they might make me more or less effective. I examine the little things that truly waste my time and are unproductive. I peer into every corner of my life. I contemplate my relationships, family, friends and business associates. I consider who can guide me: what ideas can the people close to me share that will help me be a better family man, friend and manager? What don't I know that I should know? I spend time wondering what I'm avoiding learning. I reflect on my fears. I perform a complete personal audit.

When I enter The Thinking Room on a regular basis, my business evolves, my personality shines and my family likes me a whole lot better!

If I'd had a coach or a set of tools like those I'm providing here in this book, I would have saved myself some tough times (otherwise known as the 60s, 70s and 80s)! But you don't have to suffer for your success. This book provides the techniques and the tools. You provide the faith, and you'll see your life transform.

The New System for Success:
- Work toward success like a professional football player. Reinvent yourself with each passing season.
- Create a Thinking Room or create time just for thinking.
- To compete in today's marketplace, you must be smarter and better informed.
- Put my techniques from this book to work and you will see change.

Questions for The Thinking Room:

1. Where is the perfect place for *your* Thinking Room?

2. How much time are you willing to commit to The Thinking Room? When, specifically, are you going to enter The Thinking Room?

3. Do you believe you can reinvent yourself? Why or why not?

Chapter Two

Thinking is the Hardest Thing We Do

You want to start a new business. You take out a loan. You print some business cards and letterhead. You create a webpage. How much thought did you put into it?

Thinking is the hardest thing we do.

You need to hire someone. You put out an ad. A prospect calls. He comes in for an interview. You hire him. How much thought did you put into it?

Thinking is the hardest thing we do.

You need more customers. "Advertise in our magazine. We have over 5,000 subscribers!" the ad sales representative says. You buy the advertising. How much thought did you put into it?

Thinking is the hardest thing we do.

Several months later you look up from your desk and wonder why you're not seeing any progress. You've been working hard, right?

Writer John M. Eades once admitted, "There are some days I practice positive thinking, and other days I'm not positive I am thinking."

Thinking is the hardest thing we do!

Who has Time to Think?

We have more choices than ever. At any given moment during the day, we have dozens of choices to make. And once you select which road to take, it may be years before you find out it was the wrong path. Immersing yourself in The Thinking Room forces you to harness your own brainpower to make the best decisions, now. But thinking takes time.

Microwaves, Blackberries, high-speed Internet, email, instant foods, vacuums that clean your room for you ... all designed to "save" you time. But do we have any extra time? Since you ordered the upgrade that gives you the "fastest" Internet speed, do you find that you have ten minutes more of rest or fun or productive work each day?

No, you are as busy as ever, with little time to eat a proper meal let alone find time to think.

In a click-on, click-off society, we feel that every decision has to be made right now and immediately followed up with an action. We have become accustomed to speed. We get information so quickly that we want to make decisions, make money and grow our businesses just as quickly. In the midst of all of this, there is simply no time to think.

Consider television and the brief segments that fill up our shows. The topics are rapid-fire, holding our attention for just short periods of time. Even the news has shorter segments than ever before, with more images, more graphics and more music. But what happened to the content? The American attention span is shrinking at a rapid pace.

So where do we learn how to think in an environment that seeks to all but destroy this incredibly valuable process? When we were kids our parents made all the tough decisions. In school our teachers helped with making decisions. And then the boss made all the important decisions. Have you ever been taught how to think? I know nobody taught me. After facing the consequences of living a "thoughtless" life, I began to teach myself.

When you are tempted to say, "I don't have time to think," consider the consequences. If you spent just 1% of your day (that is 14 minutes) thinking, research suggests that you will grow your income by 20%. Now do you have the time to think?

Train your Monkey

Have you ever watched a monkey? When monkeys are not trained properly, they act completely out of control. They are all over the place, jumping from one activity to the next.

You have to train your brain or it will behave similarly. When I was younger, my brain worked on monkey time. I couldn't focus. I was doing destructive things. So I began to train my monkey. Focusing your brain takes repeated efforts. You've got to read, study, and most importantly, spend time alone in contemplative thought. If you don't, the consequences are scary.

Here's an example of how difficult and yet crucial it is to take the time to think things through. I recently asked one of my consulting clients, "Why do you do what you do? Why do you hire the way you hire? Why are you advertising the way you advertise? Why do you sell what you sell?"

He had no answers.

My client was not focusing his thoughts either. He hadn't trained his monkey. And his business was wildly out of control because of it. Like so many of us, he was a reactionary. Like the untrained monkey he jumped around with no thought about each move. Many of us might recognize this behavior in our own patterns. It's tempting to forego strategy and deep thinking for the lure of a quick solution or an easy buck.

Tempting Distractions Abound

To think clearly and efficiently, you have to enter a stress-free environment. I usually get to my office at 6:00 a.m. In the quiet of the early morning, I often sit and think for ten or fifteen minutes. Just sit. Just think.

But don't get me wrong. I'm no Buddha. Temptations abound. The 47 unread emails filling my inbox demand attention. The blinking red light on my phone beckons me to check the voicemail. A stack of mail pleads to be opened. I'll admit, sometimes I give way to the busyness of business.

The average person can only remember four to seven things at a time. If you can read a list of eight or more items and recall all of them (and I mean simply by reading them once, and I'm not talking about a bulleted list of short phrases), then you're a genius. If you aren't a genius, stop trying to cram so much into your brain at one time. Slow down and think about one thing at a time.

Those ten or fifteen minutes of solitary thought radically reform the day before me. I approach those emails, voice messages and letters with a different state of mind.

I've thought about my goals. I've meditated on my purpose. I've exercised my brain. What a difference.

The Ripple Effect

What shape does a goal take when you consider it in its broadest context? Think of your goal like a pebble dropped in a still pool, gently rippling out in all directions. With your pebble as the goal, sitting solidly in the middle, the details necessary to accomplish that goal spread out around it. By taking one concrete idea and expanding upon it exponentially, you grow your goal into a fully realized set of tasks and solutions.

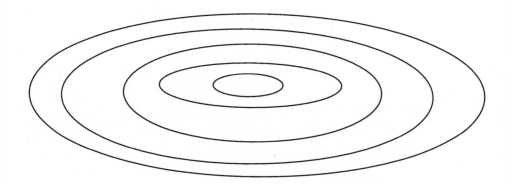

Five Ways Not to Think

But let's get real for a minute here. Most of us don't believe we have the time or capacity to think through our goals and actions in such detail. In fact, sometimes it seems as though we avoid thinking at all costs. Out of fear or laziness, we put up barriers to critical thinking. Here are five ways NOT to think:

1. Limited perspective: This is the way I see it, and I can't see beyond that.
2. Adversary thinking: He's always wrong, so I must be right. I can't agree with him.
3. Time Panic: I have to make this decision right now! There's no time to think!
4. Arrogance: There couldn't possibly any answers other than those I have already come up with.
5. Subjective: This is how I *feel* about it.

Thinking Forces you to do Research

I have a friend who is an attorney. I told him about my Thinking Room theories and he enthusiastically agreed with them. This very successful man uses Starbucks as his Thinking Room. He goes there by himself and just sits with his coffee and thinks.

"Coach, people pay me big money to do their thinking for them," he said.

"Why don't people do the thinking for themselves?" I responded.

"You mean besides the fact that I have the education, knowledge and experience they don't have?" he joked.

But then he thought about it more carefully, "People don't do their homework," he explained. "They don't do their research. They don't think about things before they get into them, and then they end up desperate for a lawyer to do the thinking for them once it's too late."

In our arrogance and limited perspective, we go through our lives believing that we have all the necessary knowledge. The problem is that you don't know what you don't know. Often, you don't know what you need to know.

When you enter The Thinking Room, you come with just one question. This one question leads to many, many more. These questions push you towards research (and by research I don't mean just a quick Google search, though that can be a good place to start).

Seek out the successful. Study the excellent books. Secure a good consultant. Most people stop trying to learn after they've secured their "dream job." Well, first of all, keep dreaming up your "dream job." Once you achieve it, re-dream the dream job. Second, making a profit today takes plenty of studying just to keep up with changing trends and technology. What are you doing to enhance your brainpower right now?

Alone with Your Thoughts

Thinking is hard for all the reasons we've discussed: we're not accustomed to it, we don't make the time, we don't have the right strategies, we never learned how and we don't have the right environment. But perhaps the most difficult part of thinking is what might happen while you are alone with your thoughts.

We all have parts of our lives we don't want to face. We have fears, doubts, painful memories, anger, hurt, embarrassment, loss and questions so big we can't even bear them. We engage in a fast life, perhaps making poor choices, so we can avoid being alone with our thoughts.

But if you really want to succeed, you must face even the most difficult thoughts. Sometimes, clear thinking requires more courage than intelligence. It's time to embrace the quiet. It's time to answer the big questions. It won't be easy, but it's time to think.

The New System for Success

- You don't have the time to think? MAKE time! It could grow your income by 20%.
- Train your monkey: Slow down and focus.
- Escape the distractions and the busyness of business for just 10 to 15 minutes each day.
- Learn to think objectively, honestly, rationally and humbly.
- Consider what your goal might look like as it expands.
- Do your research.

Questions for The Thinking Room

1. What excuses do you make for avoiding thinking?

2. Are you easily distracted? What are some ways you can reduce distractions?

3. Which of the *Five Ways Not to Think* is your greatest downfall?

4. What research do you need to do to supplement your decision-making?

Chapter Three

Where do You Get Your Information?

The old adage suggests "Seek and ye shall find." But it doesn't tell you where to do your seeking. The Internet, television, radio, friends and your employer all offer an assortment of facts and information. Who is right? Who has the best information?

Viral Information

I was at the gym the other day, enjoying a conversation with a friend. This friend was sharing his recent exchange with a multi-millionaire. This multi-millionaire insisted that real estate was on the verge of collapse. This person suggested gold as *the ultimate and wisest investment* today.

I couldn't help but think, "Where is this guy getting his information?" All of a sudden, non-facts become the next big thing.

Let's say that after the gym I trek to my local coffee shop. I run into an acquaintance and share the *gold theory* with her. Then she tells five people. One of those five people writes it on his blog. Then visitors to the blog send emails to their friends, embellishing the "dying real estate market" theory and the "billions to be made in gold." Many people will believe it and start buying up gold, without doing an ounce of research.

Research is part of thinking. Because you can think and think, but if there's no fact or foundation for those thoughts, aren't they somewhat meaningless?

So many people fail at business and life because they get their information from the wrong sources. How is your business going to succeed if your friend's sister-in-law's roommate's cousin says you should paint your store green? You must research and *you* must think for yourself.

This is how we get our information today. Instead of experts, we accept loose-lipped advice from any Joe.

Consider Wikipedia, which is an online encyclopedia where all the data is compiled by volunteers. Any person in the world can contribute information. On one hand, you get a variety of resources in an unedited format. On the other hand, who knows if anything is true? Think about your research.

The great thinker Thomas Edison said, "Our greatest need is to teach people **how to think** -- not what, but HOW." Isn't this so true? I believe our institutions have failed us completely. We've turned into a country of people who believe anything. We need to teach ourselves how to think.

When you act on uninformed decisions, you are allowing someone else to run your life. Can you believe how many people are basing their business decisions on someone else's opinion? Be your own detective. Save yourself from misinformation.

What are you Listening to?

Most of us have been brought up to be tolerant of others' viewpoints. How many times have you heard, or even said, "One person's opinion is just as good as another's"? Or "It's all just a matter of opinion"?

Well, the fact of the matter is that it isn't. Some opinions are well-formed and intelligently reasoned; others are off-the-cuff and ignorant. Some are the results of serious thought and debate; others are no more than sound bites repeated by folks who insist on using their mouths more than their heads. Tolerance means being willing to listen to others; it does not mean you have to agree with them or, after hearing their viewpoint, even take them seriously.

Those who know how to think for themselves are destined for success. These people realize that most problems are open to examination and creative solution. They immerse themselves in proper research, think about their findings and then create the most important product in today's economy: **ideas**.

However, most Americans don't know how to research and think. They are the **"idea consumers."** They let everyone else do the research for them. They may spout off shallow data or interesting anecdotes to appear intelligent. But this is not the same as using your brainpower to develop your own ideas.

These research-avoiding folks often quote "they." You know, "them."

"They say you should take Vitamin E and eat tomatoes to prevent cancer."

"They say you should invest in gold instead of real estate or stocks."

"They say you should always wear a red tie and a white shirt to interviews."

While some of these statements could be true, I ask just one question: Who in the world are THEY? Withhold your comment unless you know it to be true, and you have the source to back you up.

Once upon a time, all you had was information through word of mouth. Today is different. You have limitless information at your fingertips. When I got started in business there was no Internet. The open sharing and communication of ideas that exists today was nowhere to be found. You have no excuse for blindly following unsubstantiated advice. You have no excuse for living an uninformed life.

The Most Dangerous Source of Information: YOU

Deep within your brain sits a gigantic filing cabinet cataloguing every detail of your life. Countless files list every experience. The first time you got hired and fired, your first date, your dad's lessons on saving money, your teacher's red pen critiques on your papers, your coach's feedback on your game. Every little detail has been filed away, whether we remember it or not. It's hard to shake the lessons you've learned, even if they are all wrong.

You have a "Results" file too. Your results file is very important to you, because if you have a history of poor or just average results, then you do not know how to win. Which brings me to how *you* can often be your own worst source of information. So many of our actions are based on information we obtained at an early age. This information may or may not be accurate.

Evaluate your core beliefs about money, business, success and relationships. Is there something you need to unlearn? If you always tell yourself "I can't win" and "This is too hard." What are you listening to? Lousy self-talk is the ultimate source of wrong information.

Here is an example. There is a file labeled "Results – School." If it reads "Got mostly C's" then your file tells you that you are not a good student. It keeps you from trying hard to perform, because you believe that you are just a C student. Your file, or inner belief system, is damaged.

You need new stuff and positive additions in your school file. How can you add that to your file? Take an interesting community college class and promise yourself success. Put that "A" paper or test up on the refrigerator and give yourself a reward for finishing strong.

If your personal files are filled with negative experiences or average results, then it will be more challenging for you to add new projects to that file. If you are not used to winning and doing well, then how do you change your thinking or change your file? The best way is to start is with a small, achievable goal.

Here is another example. Public speaking scares nearly everybody, but good public speaking skills are an important aspect of business. So join a Toastmaster Club in your area and buy books or read articles about speaking. Do some homework. Learn what the experts do. Learn to practice and practice your skills. Make your initial talks to first graders, your family or friends. Make your first talks short. Learn to excel at something and this will bring you confidence.

You win by studying your inner files and discovering how *your past has been dictating your present.* Your thoughts can be the most powerful tool for change. Think about it like this: *Your thoughts lead to feelings. Feelings lead to action and the right action leads to winning results.*

The Game of Chess

I keep a chess set in my office. I love playing the game, but also, the board reminds me to approach my business with the skill of an expert chess player.

To succeed at chess, the player must think several moves in advance. They must have alternate moves planned for whatever their opponent may try. The very best players think ten to twenty moves ahead. I'm amazed at this skill!

To succeed in business, you have to plan out ten to twenty moves. Research allows you to plan the best moves in advance. Read the news. Stay caught up on the hottest trends. Take a gander at the many influential blogs out there. Study scholarly research. Subscribe to several publications in your industry. This is how you prepare like a winning chess player.

You also have to be prepared for anything! Chess players predict their opponent's moves. In the same way, think about your competition. Find out what they are doing that is really working for them. Anticipate changes in the economy, culture and community. Poor research is the real reason businesses don't survive the times.

Prepare like a chess champion, and you'll be a champion in business.

The New System for Success:

- Beware of viral information. Even if a smart person gives you information, do research to verify it.
- Don't put your trust in random people for business advice. Look to the experts and, ultimately, use your own brain to make a decision.
- Don't allow false information from your "inner files" to seep into your actions. Your inner files hold all the lessons you learned in childhood as well as your beliefs about yourself.
- Become a scholar of your business.
- Stay informed to keep ten to twenty moves ahead of your competition. Think like a chess player.
- Re-program your inner files when needed.

Questions for The Thinking Room:

1. When have you believed hearsay and the information proved invalid?

2. How are your "inner files" affecting your decision-making?

3. What are some ideas you have for getting a few moves ahead of the competition?

Chapter Four

No Time to Think?
Fire Yourself

I think I know a little bit about you. You're somebody who wants to achieve more in your life. You want to improve your current financial situation and grow your business.

You know what else? I think you're somebody with big goals and zero time to accomplish those goals. You are overwhelmed and frustrated with the day-to-day exhaustion of your work.

I think you're hoping this book is the answer to your frustration. Well, guess what? That is exactly why I wrote this book: as an answer to those frustrations.

Hope Delivered

As the president of a company that works with thousands of businesses, I have the opportunity to observe what works and what doesn't. I don't speak solely from my own experiences, but from the many lessons I've learned from my clients and colleagues. I have seen the greatest successes and the mightiest disasters.

I hate to say it, but most people should not be in business. It's an honest, somewhat tragic, thing to say. But it's true. Most people will not do their homework, or study to really learn something so that they can make a great living.

When I was young, I saved up enough money to join a country club. It was a big expense for me at the time, but I knew I would get to mingle with some very successful people.

I listened in on the conversations happening around me and took mental notes on what these successful business people said. I quickly realized that the successful people are *thinkers*. I was always impressed by their knowledge, vocabulary and dedication. I decided that I too would become a *thinker*.

Here's the problem. Business owners, managers and salespeople say they "don't have time" to think. That is why

I am telling you to fire yourself so you can spend more time in The Thinking Room.

When I say, "fire yourself," I'm saying that learning how to **delegate**, learning how to **outsource** and leverage **technology** will help grow your business in an unbelievable way. When you fire yourself, you give yourself the opportunity to *think*.

Here is an example. My friend invested a bundle of money in his new business, but he tried to get it off the ground without outside help. When the business was failing, he admitted his arrogance in believing that he could make his business profitable all on his own.

Things were not going well. He had no time to focus on his long-term goals because he was so focused on the hundreds of daily tasks he needed to complete.

I explained to my friend that his focus should be on the things that he does well, like bookkeeping, and he should get help in areas where he's weaker, like sales and marketing. I am glad to report that my friend has started to take the proper steps: **outsourcing, delegating** and **utilizing technology**.

It took some convincing, but he is now interviewing sub-contractors in the marketing business and looking for part-time sales people. Sometimes, being honest with yourself and admitting you cannot do everything alone is the first step to achieving success.

Doing "Pretty Good"

The most common downfall of small businesses can be attributed to the arrogance of the owner. When I started in the banking industry, I was shocked to see businesses fail because the owners were too prideful to admit their weaknesses. I vowed not be like that. Yet when I started my own business, I found it all too easy to slip into that same mindset I criticized.

Fortunately, my wife saved me from failure. I call her the "little brunette," because she's small but powerful. She kept insisting that I hire more experts. There were all those little things that I needed to do but kept putting on the back shelf. My wife must have told me every day for three straight years that we needed to begin outsourcing.

But, in my perspective, the company was doing "pretty good." And I would eventually get to all those tasks necessary for us to grow, right?

Wrong. Those dreams and goals just sat on shelf, gathering dust.

After three years, I finally listened to the Little Brunette! When we started to delegate tasks, our company really took off. Nations Transaction Services became a multi-million dollar business because I finally allowed myself to trust others and gave myself permission to do critical thinking and strategizing.

Are your dreams and goals gathering dust? Are you slaving away at a business that is doing *pretty good*? Is *pretty good* enough for you?

The Benefits of a Project Manager

Instead of working **in** your business, you need to work **on** your business. Start by hiring a project manager. Hire a smart, experienced individual who is very task-oriented.

Spend an extensive amount of time finding the right person for the job. Post advertisements in the paper and online. Recruit the people you meet. Ask friends and family for recommendations. Interview several people.

In the interview, mention a particular project you have your mind set on. Let's say your goal is to expand your sales territory to the next county. Ask your applicant, "What specific things would you do today to move towards that goal?" Look for creative and detailed answers. You really need someone who is confident and competent.

If he or she needs to come back to you about every decision, it's not going to work. You need to authorize your project manager to hire sub-contractors and negotiate the price. You need to authorize him or her to build strategic partnerships with vendors and sub-contractors. You need to authorize him or her to manage the details so you don't have to get involved in every little task.

It is essential that you meet with your project manager on a regular basis. Set up a weekly time for meeting and ask your project manager to give you a detailed progress report. Inspire and encourage your project manager, giving positive and honest feedback.

Multiply Yourself

In addition to hiring a project manager as a point-person, I hired more sub-contractors. I do what I do best while letting others do what they do best. There are so many experts that are just waiting for you to hire them, for a fair price. And they will help your business and personal life more than you can imagine. I have a trainer, a mentor, a website designer/manager, an editor, and dozens of other professionals. I need help with the right techniques in order to do my best in every area of work. It is a real challenge to climb a mountain alone.

So many people have great ideas, but never find the time to accomplish them because they are doing 100% of the work in their business, from bookkeeping to marketing. You must find a way to multiply yourself. If you aren't a bookkeeper, then you shouldn't be keeping the books. If you aren't a marketing professional, then you shouldn't be doing all the marketing.

I know that you're thinking, "I can't afford to hire all these people!" Well, the truth is that if you want your business to thrive, you can't afford *not* to. Begin to see outsourcing as a key component to your business, a built-in cost. The upfront costs of hiring the right people for the jobs will more than pay for themselves as you watch your business flourish.

Do what you do best. Then find others who do what they do best. Together, you will make the perfect team.

Put Technology to Work for You

The best salesperson you may ever have is the Internet. Why? It can sell and market you and your business 24 hours a day! That means you are *connecting* with others and *building relationships*, even while you are doing something else! Consider this:

While you sleep at night, a potential client is reading your blog from their home office.

While you meet with your staff, customers can make a purchase online.

While you take your kids to the park on Saturday, a customer is printing off a coupon from your website.

While you attend a conference to learn about the current developments in your industry, a customer is checking out the weekly email newsletter.

Think about it! Technology is delegation at its best.

Some of you may think that the Internet isn't a tool for your business. But if you want to compete in today's marketplace, you'd better find a way to get tech-savvy. Websites today are yesterday's yellow pages, and much more. When you have a website, it tells your customers that you understand technology, and you're ready to meet their needs.

Using the Internet is absolutely critical to your success. If your customer doesn't read the newspaper, throws out all their "junk" mail and refuses sales calls, how is your customer going to know that you exist?

And if you are not an expert at website design and website copy, you need to hire someone who is. Just as an excellent website can grow your profits, an amateur-looking website will defeat your business. The painful truth is that most small business owners do not have a clue about marketing. They have hopes. But hopes won't get the job done. Utilize technology and put its resources to work for you.

Collect Contacts

Every business and every businessperson needs to create a database. I am absolutely shocked when I walk into a store or call a business and am not asked for my email address. Developing your database can be the best thing for your business. Find a way to communicate with your customer base. Do you have the time and skills to manage a functional database and create a quality newsletter? If not, hire the professionals.

There are many companies that specialize in database management. They can set you up with a simple system that can do amazing things. You can send weekly, monthly or seasonal newsletters to your database, depending on what's right for you. Make sure your newsletter is more than an advertisement. It needs to have value for the person who opens it; otherwise they will simply delete it.

How do you add value to an email? Include interesting, easy-to-read articles. Include a printable coupon. Offer helpful advice that relates to your business. Newsletters should be about the reader, not the sender.

Find still other ways to add contacts to your database. Attend trade shows or local festivals and raffle off prizes. People can fill out a small piece of paper (where you can get more important information), or just drop in a business card. Growing your contact list is so crucial.

So now you have a database and a great website. The next step is logical. Drive your database to your website. Send out a newsletter with a creative spin. Offer a special deal if they click through the newsletter to your website. Include promotions like contests and sweepstakes. A percentage of people who receive the email will go to your website, and a percentage of those visitors will make a purchase or inquire for more information.

Congratulations! Technology has officially supplemented your sales efforts!

Finally, Time to Think

What's the best thing about delegating, outsourcing and leveraging technology? It frees you up so you can have time to be in The Thinking Room. Fire yourself! Put your trust in others who know what they are doing.

The most valuable thing I learned from athletics is how to be part of a team. I'm not the game. I'm just part of the team. I want to support my team, and take advantage of their support.

You need to develop the same attitude toward managing your business.

Once you develop this attitude, you will finally have the freedom to really think. You will find new solutions, dream new dreams, and create new opportunities. When you fire yourself, you set yourself free.

The New System for Success:
- Delegate your tasks to an all-star manager
- Outsource some of your "to-do" list to the experts
- Put technology to work for you

44

Questions for The Thinking Room

1. If you had more time, what would you do with it?

2. What tasks would you like to pass on to a qualified project manager?

3. What experts could help you in your business?

4. How can technology help you market yourself 24 hours every day?

Chapter Five

Ready for Change

Predicting the courses our lives will take is like playing weatherman. We can make our best guess about tomorrow's weather, but we have no control over it. There is no way to know for sure whether it will rain or shine. In our lives, we try to create a forecast, but we can never know exactly what the next days will bring. There is one thing, however, that we do know with absolute certainty: Change is inevitable.

How are you at adapting to change? Does the very idea of "change" make you sweat a little? Change is the basis of life. You can't avoid it. In fact, your ability to change and adapt is essential to your happiness, peace and success.

I am writing this book because I want you to know that you *can* change. I want you to know that you can change your thoughts, which will affect your attitude and actions, which will change your life.

Holding on Too Tightly

I want you to do a little exercise for me. Hold on to this book tightly. Squeeze this book in your hands as tight as you can. Are your hands and arms shaking? Is your body becoming tense?

This is what happens when you hold on to your ideas too tightly. You become filled with tension. When you hold this tightly to something, you become paralyzed and incapable of doing anything else.

Now release. There's a feeling of freedom and relief, right? Becoming *ready for change* means letting go.

People don't like change because they are afraid of it. We don't change jobs because we're afraid there might not be something better out there. We stay in bad relationships because we are afraid nobody else will love us. We stay overweight because we are too afraid of the sacrifices we will have to make to get healthy.

Why are we so full of fear? We are full of fear because we lack knowledge. We don't know how to get from Point A to Point B. The first step toward conquering fear is gaining knowledge.

How do you begin change? Assign yourself the smallest task. Break down your goal into the most manageable portions. Think about it like climbing a mountain. You just take it one step at a time.

When you are in The Thinking Room, this is not the time to hold on to your ideas with an iron grip. Release your ideas to the extent that your thinking process becomes open and flexible. If you are only making decisions based on what is directly in front of you, then you are not prepared for change.

If you hold a magazine close to your face, you can't read a thing. But if you hold it further away, now you can see it. However, if you hold it too far, you can't read it again. Entering The Thinking Room means looking at your life and business from the ideal distance. Enough distance so that the issue isn't blinding you, but not from such distance that you can simply ignore the issue.

Fearing Change

Every change you make carries a risk. When you make a decision to change some aspect of your life or business, you risk making the wrong choice. Fear of change is really a fear of risk and the unknown.

The best way to overcome your fear of change is research. My philosophy is always "Wait three days and do nothing." This phrase is a little misleading in that you're not actually "doing nothing." Instead, you're holding off on taking action until you've had some time to gather your thoughts, educate yourself, and arrive at the best conclusion. Before making a big change, take three days to research and explore that path. Despite what our urgent minds tell us, most decisions really can wait. I will discuss this further in the chapter entitled "Date your Decisions."

I Don't Have the Time

We have all been given the same amount of time in a day. Yet, why do people say, "I don't have the time."

I don't have the time for schooling.

I don't have the time to exercise.

I don't have the time to do my homework.

I don't have the time to read business books.

These are just excuses. What you're really saying is, "I don't prioritize the time, because I'm afraid of change." There are many different approaches that you can take toward change. It's up to you to select the path that enhances your success.

When you are open to change, people will see your fresh approach. In The Thinking Room you can reinvent yourself. You can be greater tomorrow simply by changing your thoughts. When you learn to embrace change and expect more from yourself, you influence every task that follows.

In your Thinking Room sessions, write down all the little ways you want to change. Write down all the resistance you have toward change.

The Perfect Approach

My wife is my partner, and I give her a lot of credit for my success. She was always that little voice that kept saying to me, "There must be a better way." My wife would say, "We're working too hard and not getting anywhere!"

I learned the hard way that the perfect approach began with flexibility. I had to lay aside my pride and try something different. You may be surprised to learn that your biggest obstacle is YOU. This isn't meant to be an insult or to downplay your many strengths and talents. The fact is that YOU are simply in the way.

YOU aren't willing to change.

Everybody is searching for the magic solution that will grow their company and improve sales. Well here is the truth: there is no magic. There is a solution and it is called flexibility. That's how we transformed our company,

Nations Transaction Services, Inc. into a multi-million dollar business. We were willing to change with the times. Many of our peers didn't adapt to the Internet era. But I chose to leverage the Internet's resources, and it helped both our company and our clients become more successful.

If you aren't willing to change, you just won't make it.

Reactionary vs. Adapter

Do you find yourself reacting or adapting to new, challenging, or uncertain circumstances? If you're an adapter, you confront the new situation and find a way to work with the current reality. Even if you don't like it, you'll ask yourself, "How do I deal with this new reality? Can I find a way to work with it, around it, or even use it to my advantage?" If you're an adapter, then you're ahead of the game! You understand the power of flexibility and the inevitability of change.

But what if you're a reactionary? Don't be ashamed to admit it. Many of us are easily set off by a small change in plans or an uncertain situation. The problem is that when you react negatively, you impact your life and your business decisions before giving yourself the opportunity to adapt.

Change is inevitable. So if you're the type of person who flies into a tailspin every time life throws you a curveball, it stands to reason that you won't easily succeed. No wonder so many people aren't working to the best of their abilities. They are swimming in a pool of negativity. Instead of thinking about the challenge and putting it into perspective, they *react* and *resist*.

Instead of reacting to the situations around you, enter The Thinking Room and figure out how to adapt. If you can be an adapter instead of a reactionary, I guarantee you will see greater success in your life.

Resistance builds Persistence

I keep weights in my office, both as exercise equipment and as a visual reminder of resistance. The first time I lifted that 20 pound weight I thought, "There's no way I can work out with this." Too much resistance. But when someone trained me with the proper techniques and I worked my way up to 20 pounds, the resistance wasn't so tricky. With training, you can accommodate the resistance, and even conquer it.

In the end, the resistance made me stronger. Think about it. Does resistance scare you? Well, guess what? Resistance is the only path to strength.

The people in our society who arrive at the top of their field have usually faced the most resistance. Consider a brain surgeon. The brain surgeon has to accomplish undergraduate studies, take the MCATs, attend medical school, and complete their internship and residency. Meanwhile, they must find a way to fund their expensive education, work ridiculous hours and learn the most complicated curriculum. Now that's a lot of resistance. But their persistence wins the battle. And it is that persistence that allows them to carry out some of the most intricate, life-saving procedures known to modern medicine. It is that persistence that allows them to spend twelve hours in surgery and save hundreds of lives during their career.

There has not been one expert surgeon, great athlete or self-made millionaire that has not faced resistance in their life. It is the difference-maker for anyone that has not reached their goals. If you are facing resistance in your life, don't look at it as a setback. Instead, consider it a strength-builder. Tweak, change, try a different approach, study and train. Are you ready for change?

The New System for Success:
- You can change. Learn how to become an adaptable person.
- If you hold on too tightly to your ideas, then you won't be ready for newer, better ideas.
- Don't make excuses. Your excuses are just cover-ups for your fears. Face your fear of change instead of ignoring it.
- Resistance makes you strong. Persist in spite of the struggles.

Questions for The Thinking Room:

1. How adaptable are you? When have you adapted poorly to a new environment or person?

2. What change is happening around you that makes you want to resist? Is it a new colleague, a location change, aging, developments in your industry?

3. Who is the most adaptable person you know? What do they do that works?

Chapter Six

Think about Solutions

When it comes to problems, what do we seek above all else? *Solutions.*

We seek *solutions* for the challenges in our relationships, finances, business and health. One common misconception is that an idea constitutes a solution. An idea is not a solution. Come up with 50 ideas and perhaps you discover one or two solutions among them. This is why The Thinking Room concept challenges you to take the time to find *real* solutions.

Without *The Thinking Room*: We experience a challenge. We ask a friend for advice. Maybe we frantically use Google or Wikipedia in search of the answer. Perhaps we spend little to no time at all searching for a solution. But let's assume our friend does deliver on that advice. With little of our own research we find ourselves cheering, "The solution!" The first solution serves as the "winning" solution simply because it's the first idea we've come across. We grab the low-hanging fruit and immediately apply it to the challenge. Mission accomplished, right?

Using *The Thinking Room* Concept: We experience a challenge. We spend significant time recognizing the challenge, questioning the challenge, dissecting the challenge. We seek advice from wise mentors. We arrive at a solution, but we don't stop there. We consider numerous other solutions and from this pool we select the best. Perhaps this takes us a week rather than a few hours. This time, *mission truly accomplished.*

Winning Solutions Begin with Perseverance

It is so easy to become frustrated by obstacles. If you are striving for success, I can guarantee that you will be confronted with setbacks. I can guarantee that you will become frustrated. I can guarantee that you will experience such grave discouragement that you won't want to continue on the path to success.

But a setback doesn't actually have to set you back. In fact, it often provides the perfect opportunity for advancement if you're willing to use it as an exercise in perseverance.

There is only one approach to frustration and disappointment: never give up. I don't think I'm the smartest guy or even the savviest, but the one character trait I have in abundance is perseverance. In fact, I'm so persistent it can be annoying (or so I've been told)!

Beginning in my teens and twenties, I observed that *perseverance* was the ultimate skill required for success. Even during the toughest days in my troubled childhood, I kept working toward a better life. During the most challenging seasons of starting a business, I pressed toward my goal to be a leader in the bankcard industry. And throughout my most exhausting days at the office, I keep my promise to spend time in The Thinking Room.

On my office desk I have an authentic green cast iron pump. It reminds me to keep priming the pump. As your business or career is growing, you need to keep pumping.

Once a business has grown and becomes very successful, many people may let up on the amount of work they put in. If you want to continue to see results and keep your business or career growing, you can never stop pumping the hard work. A successful business or career should give you a reason to work even harder and be even more creative.

I know how to prime the pump. With over 35 years spent working with thousands of merchants, I have the creative ideas and business tools necessary to help grow a business. The pump reminds me that we are never really "finished", even when we achieve success.

The first thing I look at when I coach somebody is their history of perseverance. To achieve better solutions in your business and life, you absolutely need this quality. If you want to scare the failure right out of your life, practice the virtue of persistence.

Get Un-Frustrated by Counting to 10

So now you're ready to persevere despite an apparent obstacle. You may wonder what concrete techniques you can employ to get yourself on the right track?

I have a specific method for finding better solutions. When confronted with a setback, I *Count to 10 and Win*.

Using this exercise, I have tackled hundreds of dilemmas in my life and business. Whether I am starting with a goal, a problem, a decision or a question, I turn to this exercise. In fact, this is how I problem-solve with my consulting clients.

For me, seeing something on paper helps me grasp the situation. I find that seeing a physical example helps my clients to turn an abstract idea into a concrete idea.

I begin by thinking about how I can accomplish my goals. I think about all the possibilities and all the things that have challenged me concerning this goal. After considering my goals and frustrations for a day or two, I turn my thoughts into a writing exercise.

I begin by making a simple chart. I create ten rows and ten columns. Across the ten columns I write ten goals, ideas or solutions.

Let's use the example of a pet grooming business. I've never had a pet grooming business, but for the sake of argument let's assume I do. And let's say my pet grooming business is not generating the best profit. Here is how I would start the *Count to 10 and Win* chart.

Get new customers	Expand the business to include more variety	Offer services to Veterinarians	Reduce expenses	Retain customers	Raise prices	Upsell grooming services	Create a presence in community	Franchise	Sell business

Okay, I've got ten across. Now I want to go ten deep. Sometimes I can't quite go ten across *and* ten deep, but I do the best I can.

Get new customers	Expand the business	Offer services to Veterinarians	Reduce expenses	Retain customers	Raise prices	Upsell grooming services	Create a presence in community	Franchise	Sell business
Advertise in local paper	Pet sitting	Dr. Smith	Bring on interns	Monthly newsletter	10% increase in January	Upgraded products	Sponsor events	Sell locally	Talk to business brokers
Mass postcard mailer	Pet massage	Dr. Jones	Buy soap in higher bulk	Loyalty card program	$1 more per grooming	Optional organic products	Donate gift cards to fundraisers	Sell online	$25,000 potential sale
Door hangers in neighborhood	Simultaneous owner and pet spa treatments	Dr. Brown	Evaluate insurance	Survey customer on satisfaction		Add on a special treat for pet	Talk to schoolkids about pets	Talk to lawyer	$15,000 debt to pay off
Coupons published in mailers	Bird grooming	Emergency Pet Clinic		Thank you gifts for owners		Accessories	Write articles about pets		$10,000 potential profit
Join community groups	Pet transport			Accept credit cards		Conditioning products	Join community groups		
Marketing piece at pet stores	Gourmet pet foods								
Referral bonus for current customers	In-home or on-sight pet grooming								

It takes time, but in the end I have exhausted every possible solution. But I don't put away that pen yet; I'm not done!

I then draw out dozens of boxes on a fresh piece of paper. I begin to pull out the most significant findings of *The Count to 10 and Win* chart.

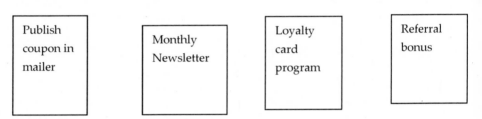

Then I break down each box into more specific tasks. I take each box and spend as long as I can, coming up with as many as possible. I may have 10 squares, or 50 squares or 100 squares. I just keep breaking the boxes down into smaller ideas and tasks. For example:

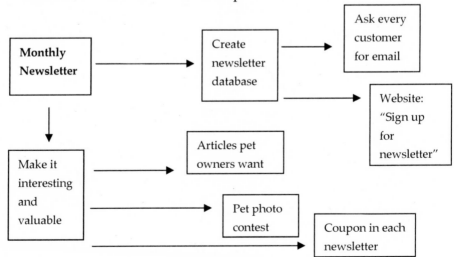

It's a lot like putting a puzzle together. I add one piece at a time until the clear, full picture begins to emerge. With these small steps lined up for me, my challenges start to become opportunities.

What once seemed like an insurmountable obstacle has now been broken down into easily accomplishable tasks. It becomes obvious where each puzzle piece is going to fit, and I begin to work with greater speed and confidence. I am finally un-frustrated and the real fun can begin.

Most people focus only on the goal, instead of on the present task. They work hard, spend too much time and money on their big dream, but never accomplish anything. By breaking down the goal into manageable tasks, it becomes reachable.

You can use *Count to 10 and Win* for anything. You can apply this concept to virtually any area of your life that needs enhancing. Create a *Count to 10 and Win* chart for your career, business, relationships, finances, health goals and more.

Try incorporating this exercise into your Thinking Room sessions and you'll be amazed at how much more productive your time becomes. The Thinking Room is the best place to think of creative solutions.

The New System for Success:

- Understand that everyone becomes frustrated and experiences setbacks. The difference between winners and losers is that winners persevere despite setbacks.
- When overwhelmed, make a *Count to 10 and Win* chart by coming up with 10 goals or solutions, and then as many as 10 ideas to attach to those 10 solutions.
- Break each solution into small, manageable tasks. Write them down in little boxes, making each solution feel concrete and manageable.
- Keep your goals in mind, but don't forget to focus on the present task as well.

Questions for the Thinking Room:

1. What challenge in your life would benefit from *Count to 10 and Win?*

2. When have you become frustrated with something and made a hasty decision? What were the effects?

3. Why does breaking solutions down into smaller tasks help you accomplish your goals?

4. Do you persevere in the face of obstacles? What can you do to grow the character trait of perseverance?

Chapter Seven

Moving from Thinking to Understanding

I have been amused as I watch my four-year-old granddaughter learn to tie her shoes. She's just so excited to learn! Even though it's hard work for her, she'll keep trying and trying. Wow! Remember when learning something new used to be fun?

As you become a better thinker, I want you to turn your thoughts into understanding. Understanding is when you really grasp the thought and put it into action. Understanding is applying what you learn, and guess what? It can be fun!

Learning Something New

Anything can be learned. You don't believe me? I've seen it with my own eyes: *anything* can be learned.

A physical education teacher shared an interesting story about a college class she took. In order to remind these teachers-in-training that kids will feel that they "just can't do it," the professor gave them all a very difficult task. They had to learn how to wiggle their ears. Naturally, they all said, "That's impossible! Either you're born with that ability or you aren't!"

The professor reminded them that the students will respond the same way when told to jump a hurdle, complete a mile-long run, shoot a basketball or juggle beanbags.

"Well, did you ever learn how to wiggle your ears?" I asked her.

She wiggled her ears. I was very impressed. It took her hours and hours of studying her facial muscles and practicing in a mirror.

I want you to take on a similar task in your life. Try something radically different. If you are right-handed, write with your left hand for the day. (Or vice-versa.) Or try driving home a different way for the entire week. Hold your fork in your non-dominant hand when you eat.

In doing this, you're assigning small tasks to your brain, letting it know that change is possible and that new things can be learned. Achieving small tasks forces your brain into cooperation mode.

Each time you try something new and conquer it, the little voice that says, "I can do it," becomes louder and more confident. This is how my granddaughter feels when she ties her shoes by herself.

"Grandpa! I did it!" she says with a giggle, as she points to her carefully tied shoelace.

She feels good about herself, and that confidence will carry her as she learns how to read. The confidence from knowing how to read will help her have the confidence to learn basic math. That confidence will help her to learn more and more.

Once you've gained your confidence, you are ready to turn *thinking* into *understanding*, and *understanding* into *results*. You have mastered small tasks and now you can assign bigger tasks in order to achieve your goals.

Understanding is Clarity

Thinking must lead to *understanding*. I have another activity that creates a visual examples to invisible situations.

In this exercise, I want you to think of a particular life situation. Rank it with a number between 1 and 10, with 1 being the best and 10 as the worst.

For example, "I'm really broke," is probably a 10. Your goal may be to become wealthy, a number 1. You will also rank yourself, or the qualities you posses, on the other side of the char. Rank the abilities you have to conquer your problems. Here's an example:

Life Situations	Me
1. (Goal: Financial Success)	1. Great education
2.	2. Outgoing personality
3.	3. Several good contacts
4.	
5.	
6.	
7.	
8.	
9.	
10. Reality: Totally broke	

Study this chart as a way to understand where your problems fit into the larger context of your goals and abilities. You'll gain a greater understanding on your own capacity to conquer your problems and achieve your goals. When you look at this chart, you can see that you have so much potential to overcome challenges. This is a perfect activity to take on in The Thinking Room.

Results Requires Understanding

I want a job I love.
I want to live in a better neighborhood.
I want to send my kids to the best schools.
I want my employees to work together.
I want to go back to college.

We all have things we so desperately want.

But if you only think about the **results**, you'll never see them. If you only think about having a job you love, and you don't think about the tasks required to get a job you love, then you are not in The Thinking Room. You are in the Daydreaming Room! Though it's great to reflect on the life you want, wishing and hoping won't get you there.

Focus on the details. Focus on your techniques. If you are good enough, the results (the career, business, house, money and lifestyle) will follow.

Let's say you want a new job. Write down the tasks you must do in order to get a new job. You need a new suit. You need a great resume. You need interview skills. You need to network. Focus on these tasks. Take them one at a time and think about them. Break them down into even smaller, more manageable tasks.

"Today I will go down to the suit outlet and just see what they have."

Don't rush the task. Think about it. Do some research. Look at the suits they offer and compare prices. This is the *understanding*. This is the *NOW*.

Understanding is Linked to Action

The wise man thinks before acting and the fool thinks after it. Which approach best describes you?

If you saw a fire, you'd grab the extinguisher and put it out. But you didn't think about it right then; you thought about it long before. You understood what would be expected of you in the case of an emergency. You were prepared! You bought the extinguisher. You read the directions. You placed it in a wise spot. The THINKING happened with all the preparation. The UNDERSTANDING happened when you put out the fire. You must have both. Make sense?

You must prepare for a job interview in the same way. You've worn your best suit. You've practiced eye contact and hand-shaking. You've spiffed up your resume. You've thought of some questions to ask. This is the thinking that went into your preparation for the interview.

If you invested time in The Thinking Room, you've prepared several steps further. You've anticipated the hardest questions your interviewer could ask. You've contemplated your reaction should they make an offer.

During your interview, you will understand the purpose of this thinking. You will put your thoughts into action. This is how you will see change in your life: marrying together thinking and understanding. Preparation and action. This brings results.

Thinking as Practice for Real Life

When I practice my skills on the driving range, sand bunkers and putting green, I play so much better in competition. During this concentrated practice, I absorb the subtle things that I often overlook during a round of golf. Business is similar. You need to practice!

I do not see people practice in business. I see people interested in other things like planning their vacation or day off or figuring out how to do less but make more. Here's what most people think about:

The American Idol finale is tonight...I wonder who will win. Hmm ... who should I vote for?

Where should I go to lunch today? Maybe I want seafood. No, Italian. No, maybe I want to go to that new place.

I need a new haircut. When should I schedule that for?

Most people do not win in business because they don't use their thinking time as practice for real life. Instead of allowing yourself to get easily sidetracked by the more trivial stuff, spend more time thinking about your goals, techniques and strategies.

That's not to say you can't spend some of your down time considering the fun stuff. Of course there will be times during your day when you'll be tempted to think about what's for lunch.

But see what happens if you try redirecting your thoughts. Rather than thinking about your upcoming vacation, think about your upcoming meeting. Rehearse your presentation; go over your notes. Imagine what points your coworkers might bring up, and practice your comments and feedback. This is practice. If challenging situations arise, you've already mentally prepared yourself.

Again, this is how you can turn thinking into understanding.

Your Mountain

Everybody has a personal mountain to climb. When you set out on your hike, you may be lacking faith. You look up at the enormous mountain and think, "I can never climb that!" Your perception is that you have to go straight up to get to the top.

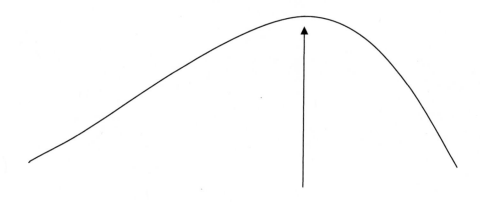

Perception: My only way to the top of this mountain is to go straight up.

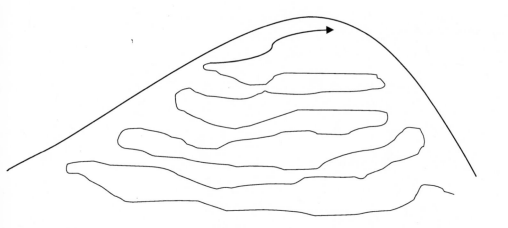

Reality: Getting up the huge mountain means walking a curved path. It's much easier, but it takes longer.

You wouldn't set out on a climb without preparation, right? You need a map, the right shoes, emergency equipment, food, water and a backpack. Your *metaphorical* mountain climb needs the same preparation and attention to detail. When you go to "hike" your mountain, you will use *understanding* to act on everything you had thought about in preparation.

With this approach, change is possible. *Change is the marrying of thinking and understanding.* Make these two virtues a priority in your life, and you will see the results you've always dreamed of.

The New System for Success

- Assign small tasks that require you to try something different, such as driving home from work a different way or writing with your non-dominant hand.
- Create a Situations vs. Assets chart to analyze your life with accuracy.
- Thinking is the preparation; Understanding is the NOW.
- Climbing a mountain requires preparation and careful thought. Don't become overwhelmed with the idea of going straight to the top.

Questions for the Thinking Room:

1. How do challenges make you feel?

2. What do you think is the difference between thinking and understanding?

3. What "mountain" in your life is intimidating? What strategies can you implement to ease the climb?

Chapter Eight

Think Week

Our lives are filled with noisy buzz. Your to-do list is part of the noise. Your cell phone is part of the noise. Your television is part of the noise. This constant noise produces apathy because it's hard to think in the midst of it. Consider how apathetic we've become as a nation. Only 60% of eligible voters in the United States even participate in national elections. We have just stopped caring.

When theologian and physician Albert Schweitzer was asked what's wrong with the world, he replied, "They don't think enough." Thinking is the highest faculty of the human mind and the key to all progress.

Yet people continue to go, go, go. It seems more important to keep moving than to stop and think.

Have you ever driven from Point A to Point B and remembered absolutely nothing about the drive? Your brain was literally on cruise control right along with your car. And guess what? For many of us it doesn't stop with the car. We are on autopilot throughout much of our waking lives.

Stuck in the Ditch

Why are we on autopilot? Because we do the same things day in and day out! We fail to vary our routine. We lose passion for our goals. We fall into a rut. And that rut turns into a ditch. Before you know what has happened, you are tired and stale. You are stuck. You are in life's ditch, and you hardly even noticed.

The ditch is seven or eight feet deep, so you are definitely trapped. Do you give up and simply "make do" in the ditch? Or do you find a way out?

If you want to get out of the ditch, you can *think* your way out. You can *think* of several solutions. You can scream and maybe a passerby will come. You can dig a ladder into the side of the ditch. There are solutions to just about any problem you may experience.

When it comes to life's ditch, an extended amount of thinking time is needed. This type of rut requires a larger commitment than just 10 minutes in The Thinking room before work. It's a bigger, more complex problem and therefore requires a bigger more complex effort on your part. But the solution is right around the corner, and it is waiting for you during *Think Week*.

The Escape

I hope I've convinced you of the importance of visiting The Thinking Room on a daily basis. But wait until you see the tremendous growth you'll experience if you offer yourself an annual *Think Week*.

On average, US workers get 13 days of vacation time. And half of all US citizens *never* use their vacation time. When they finally do get a break, they are usually tethered to their cell phone and Blackberry. Trust me, if you don't take your chance to get away and think then you limit your potential for success.

Your vacation time doesn't always have to be about lying in the sun reading a novel. If you're feeling stuck, your vacation time might be the perfect opportunity to instigate a Think Week. If you can't afford an entire week away, then just escape for a few days or a long weekend (a partial Think Week).

I've always enjoyed reading Henry David Thoreau, because I'm so fascinated with his reclusion. He literally went into the woods to escape society.

"He enjoys true leisure who has had time to improve his soul's estate," Thoreau said. This he learned from experience. Your leisure time, and the rest of your life, is enhanced by time spent in contemplation.

I want to know, have you gone into the forest? The expression, "You can't see the forest through the trees" is particularly relevant to this discussion. We have a very difficult time seeing the big picture because we are so overwhelmed with the details of life.

Maybe you can't build a cabin on Walden Pond, but I bet you could take a week away to think. Find an inspirational place that suits you perfectly. For me, I love Monterey or Tahoe. But it's about each of us finding the most relaxing and inspiring location for our own needs. It's even possible to discover new scenery, new people, different topography and different food just an hour's drive away! When you immerse yourself in a different environment, it wakes up your senses and prepares your brain for new thoughts.

Getting away also helps to slow down your process. In relative seclusion, you are better able to think clearly and be receptive to creative thoughts. As I have learned to slow down my own process, to take extended periods in The Thinking Room, I've found a happier, better existence. I have better relationships. I'm making more money. I have more peace.

Once you've decided on a location, there are just a couple of simple tools to remember: You'll just need a pad of paper and a pen. Writing things down is essential. Allow yourself to have a free flow of thoughts on paper. This is critical to a successful Think Week.

A Successful Think Week

About seven years ago, I had to make some tough decisions about growing my company. I was becoming increasingly aware of the Internet's potential to make or break our business.

So here I am in my 50s and not a technocrat by any stretch of the imagination, but I knew I was missing something. A lot of friends in my generation or older just didn't want to conform. They didn't even have a computer in their office! I didn't want to be "stuck" like them. I realized that technology was becoming the foundation for every successful business.

I needed to get away and think. I went to Tahoe for a week, with the intention of growing some new ideas. I turned off my cell phone, relaxed and pulled out my pen and paper. During that time, I brainstormed about the potential power of the Internet and what specific tasks I needed to initiate. I realized that if I wanted to compete with other businesses, I needed serious help. I came back home and hired an IT person who began by teaching me how to use my own computer!

That was just the first step, but my successful Think Week was the beginning of technological awareness. My business would never have succeeded if it weren't for this mindset shift. Today I consider myself very knowledgeable in the area of Internet sales and marketing. And I owe it all to my Think Week.

The Evaluation (A Think Week Exercise)

How many of us can say we are truly content? How many of us can say we are in harmony? Not many.

Take time out to think. Evaluate everything.

In order to gain true perspective, I try to take myself to a different emotional elevation. From this vantage point I can look down at my life, just as if I were on the mountain's peak looking down at the forest. How does the forest look? If each area of your life were a tree, which trees are healthy and growing? Which trees are bare and lifeless?

Evaluate each area of your life: your speech, your behavior, your compassion, your confidence and the list goes on and on. In fact, create your own list of "trees." Write a list of 10, 20 or 100 areas of your life that you want to evaluate, and then spend your Think Week coming up with an "idea" for each "tree." Attach a task that will turn the *idea* into an *action*. Think of it like filling out a report card for yourself. I hope you brought lots of paper!

I started the practice of "Think Week" early in my career. During one of those thinking sessions of my youth, I realized I needed to improve my communication skills. One of the best gifts I could give to others was learning to communicate. As a salesman, I needed to pronounce words properly, and use language to build bridges of hope and faith. I needed to deliver my message with the greatest confidence. As my speech improved, my career and personal life improved.

This is your opportunity to fill out a report card for yourself. How do you rate yourself in regards to relationships, family, parenting and friendship? How do you rate yourself in financial management, organization, motivation and knowledge of your trade?

And finally, what is really, really, really important to you? For me, it's not money. It's about being the best husband, father, grandfather and co-worker. For me, what's genuinely most important is that I help others to do better in their lives.

What's important to you?

Your *Think Weeks* are your unique opportunity to ask yourself this ultimate question.

Time-outs are Good for You

The Think Week theory reminds me of my wife giving time-outs to our children when they were young.

"Johnny, you need a time-out. I want you to go to your room and think about what you've done." *Think about what you've done.* Mothers get it, don't they? How lucky you are if you had a mother who gave you time-outs to *think about what you've done.*

That, my dear reader, is a practice to carry on for the rest of your life.

Think Week can lead to dreaming, goal-setting and inspiration. Think Week can literally lead you to a new life. I believe you can find yourself through the thinking process. You can think your way to self-realization and success. You can think your way to a life of peace.

Can you change the world? Maybe or maybe not. But you can and will change your own life, and that, in its own way, does change the world a little.

Take time for yourself. Take a Think Week.

The New System for Success:

- We can get stuck in life's ditch, but fresh thinking will get you out.
- Use your time off as time to think.
- Look at your life from a different elevation and evaluate your growth.
- Bring a journal with you on your Think Week, and write down everything you think about during your times personal evaluation.
- Think Week is like a corporate retreat for one.
- Think Week is like taking a time out to *think about what you have done.*

Questions for The Thinking Room:

1. Are you stuck in a ditch? How did you end up in the ditch?

2. When was the last time you took time for an extended period of thinking? What did you gain from that time?

3. Where are some places you would like to take a Think Week?

4. What are 10 areas of your life you want to evaluate during your Think Week?

Chapter Nine

Date your Decisions

How do you know when you're making the right choice? How do you know when to quit doing something that's not working? How do you know which path to take, when it comes to making important life decisions?

The Big Decisions

Certain decisions we know are big: getting married, buying a house, having a child. You put considerable thought into big decisions.

When buying a home, you think about the style, you assess what you can afford, you carefully select a real estate agent, and you visit many open houses before deciding.

Before getting married, you date that person, you really get to know them, you meet their family and then you get engaged. Hopefully at that stage you've discussed important things like career goals, financial concerns, children and religious beliefs. Most couples take at least a year before tying the knot. These are two of life's biggest decisions, but we're also faced with a multitude of other important choices each day, month and year of our lives. It worries me that so many people are either "indecisive" or just plain bad at making decisions.

At the heart of the issue is your ability to honestly rate your decisions.

How many categories do you have in your life? What about sub-categories? Are you thinking, "Is this what I want to do with my life?" You have many decisions to make. How much time are you spending thinking about your decisions, both large and small? Where do you find the time to consider these life-altering choices? In the Thinking Room.

Most big decisions scare us just enough to make us do our homework. Buying a home is a major financial commitment. Marriage is a financial, emotional and physical commitment. Even if you're not the type of person to spend extensive time making decisions, you probably know that it's wise to put time and energy into things like marriage and home buying.

But do you put enough thought and research into your business and career decisions?

You would date someone before marrying them, wouldn't you? Well, I want you to date every decision before you commit. You can think of it as "dating" or being "engaged" to your decision: You get to know it, try it on, and see it how influences the other areas of your life.

Once you've dated your decision and become comfortable with its repercussions, then you're ready to commit, or break it off.

The Experience Bank

Our decisions can only be as smart as our experiences. This is why I put so much emphasis on your experience bank. This bank is the most important one you'll ever invest in. Seriously! Your experience bank can make you richer than any 401k, CD or mutual fund. Your experience bank makes you who you are.

If you want to change your life, change your experience bank.

Do you check the balance of your checking account every day? Well, how often do you check the balance of your experience bank account? If your experience bank is full of negative experiences, then when you make a withdrawal, that currency won't be worth much.

As a young man I did not have a high-quality experience bank because I did not have a nurturing childhood. But what I did have was my athletics along with some great coaches. I was fortunate enough to learn how to commit and cooperate. Athletics taught me how to ask for help and how to build trusting relationships with others. I began to take my zero balance bank account and make small, hopeful deposits.

Sports helped, but my experience bank was still lacking. This caused me to make some poor decisions along the way. I didn't trust myself when I was young. I wasn't comfortable in my own skin, and I was too tentative to make firm decisions.

Yet, I was determined to grow my account. Fortunately I had some very successful employers who gave me incredible guidance and improved my experience bank. Over the years I've learned to seek advice and support in my decision-making.

But you want to carefully choose advisors and partners. If you are trying to make a decision about family, and you talk to your sibling (who grew up in the same dysfunctional family), is that the wisest advisor? Perhaps a counselor or therapist would be a better alternative. Learn to be humble, and ask for help from somebody with a different, healthier perspective. In some cases, there's no better investment than hiring a professional for their advice.

Based on *your* personal experience bank, what sort of professional perspective do you need? If you never learned how to manage money, consider talking to a financial advisor and accountant. If your childhood was spent in front of the TV, with no physical exercise or sports, and you have no idea how to get in shape, then hire a physical trainer.

If you have no experience in business, but want to turn your Great Idea into millions, seek out a good business consultant. There are professionals to help us supplement our experience banks: consultants, clergy, therapists, life coaches, and trainers. Also, there are books, magazines, websites, seminars, classes, clubs, support groups, nonprofits and more with the resources needed to enhance your account.

Don't be afraid to seek out these resources. You might be relieved to know that you don't have to make every decision on your own. If your experience bank is low on funds, then borrow from another person's bank and watch your own begin to grow!

Rate the Decision

Now that you have the resources to make wise decisions, take a moment to assess their place in the larger picture. Before you stress out about a decision, consider its significance. Be honest with yourself. On a scale of 1 – 10, how important is this decision? If it is low on the scale, then don't spend too much of your emotional capital worrying about it. Take a few moments of quiet reflection, and make the best decision you can.

Conversely, if it's high on the scale, invest some serious time in making that decision. Don't take the big decisions lightly, and don't allow the little decisions to obscure the larger picture. Prioritize your decision-making, and you'll feel more in control of the process.

How do you know how to rate each decision? Start by considering the possible consequences. Will it affect your personal life or your business or both? Will it hurt others' feelings or finances? Will it be positive or negative for your image? Will it help or harm your community? If your answer to most of these questions is "no" then it's probably lower on the scale. If the decision does involve some of these far-reaching consequences, then it ranks higher on the scale. How important is any given decision? You are the ultimate judge.

Investing in Others' Experience Bank

Let's talk about building the experience banks of others. Let's say you've worked hard at investing in your own experience bank and improving your decision-making ability, but your family, staff or coworkers still have crummy experience banks.

If you have children, are you building a rich and full experience bank for them? You can do this by exposing your children to diverse activities: sports, hobbies, clubs, education, travel, and literature. This is the best inheritance they could ever receive! If your children have a full experience bank, they will go farther in their lives than any of their peers, both personally and professionally.

Are you investing in the experience banks of your employees or coworkers? If you want the maximum results from your team, then each player needs a full experience bank. There are a number of ways to accomplish this. You can accompany or send them to conferences, bring in special speakers or coordinate team-building efforts. A certain Fortune 500 company requires that their employees spend thirty minutes each day reading. They can choose from an assortment of books from the company's library.

Encourage the people around you by giving them opportunities to try new things. Maybe your accounting department needs to spend a day working in the product development department. With each new encounter, their experience banks grow.

Wait Three Days and Do Nothing

Before you make an important decision, there's a process. First, you have an idea. Then you have a choice to make: do it now, do it later, don't do it, etc. In your decision-making process, do you get help?

I think people make decisions too quickly. They don't invest enough time. Learn to wait three days and do nothing. It is a principle I live by.

When someone asks you a difficult question, it is okay to say, "That is a good question. Can I do some research and get back to you?"

When someone makes an offer or a proposal, even it seems like a great deal, it is perfectly acceptable to respond with, "Thank you for the offer. It sounds great! I'd like to take a few days to think about it. Can I get back to you on Monday?" Most people will not only allow you this time, they'll respect you for taking it.

You must measure the value of each decision. Then you must measure your own ability to make that decision. Check the "available funds" in your experience bank before deciding. Ask yourself, "Does my experience bank prove that I am capable of making the best decision in this situation?" If your experience bank is low on "funds" then take out a loan from someone else.

Armed with a cohesive decision-making process, you are now on the path to making better choices and crafting a better life.

The New System for Success:

- You need to take time to make the big decisions.
- You must *rate* and *date* each decision.
- Your decisions can only be as smart as your experiences. Build your experience bank to improve your decision-making skills.
- Once you've spent time in The Thinking Room, have confidence in your decision.
- Become an investor in the experience banks' of others.

Questions for The Thinking Room:

1. What are some big decisions you've aced?

2. What are some big decisions you've failed?

3. In what areas of your experience bank do you need supplementing?

4. In whose experience bank do you need to invest? Your kids? Your employees? Your grandkids? Your friends?

Chapter Ten

Exercise your Brain

If you want to see even better results from your time in The Thinking Room, then you need to exercise your brain.

Not surprisingly, the same advice that we follow to achieve physical fitness applies to mental fitness: use it or lose it. Just as daily weight repetitions in the gym or jogging strengthen certain muscle groups, mental exercises will strengthen and enhance cognitive functions over time. The experts at MyBrainTrainer.com gave me some interesting information on this subject.

I want you to start thinking of your brain as an important muscle to keep in shape. Find ways to improve your memory and decision-making skills.

Use it or Lose it

The human brain is a remarkable organ. It consists of hundreds of billions of brain cells (neurons) and thousands of trillions of connections (synapses). Until recently, conventional wisdom held that you were born with all the brain cells you would ever have, and you would lose a significant number of these cells as you age.

Fortunately, new and improved techniques for cell counting have proven the conventional wisdom wrong. In the absence of degenerative neurological diseases such as Alzheimer's, we do not lose brain cells in significant numbers, and even the aging brain is capable of generating new cells.

Exercising your brain increases your ability to:

- process information quickly
- complete more decision cycles per fixed unit of time
- perform multiple tasks simultaneously
- retrieve old information more rapidly
- learn new information more easily
- concentrate in the presence of distractions

Stay Sharp

There are many things you can do to keep your mind sharp. Here are a few things I have learned that will improve your perception of all five senses:

Sight: Each day, observe an object (a photograph, for example) or a person you pass on the street. Draw it (or him or her) immediately. This exercises short-term memory. At the end of the week, redraw the seven objects or persons you have observed. This exercises long-term memory.

Smell/Taste: When dining in a restaurant or at a friend's home, try to identify the ingredients in the dishes you are served. Concentrate on the subtle flavorings of herbs and spices. Ask the waiter or your host to verify your perceptions.

Hearing: On the telephone, practice recognizing callers before they identify themselves. Then memorize callers' phone numbers. At the end of the day, write down the people you have spoken with that day, as well as their phone numbers. At the end of the week, try writing down as many of these as you can.

Smell/Touch: Exercise your senses of smell and touch by trying to identify objects with your eyes closed.

Simple Things that Improve your Mind

There are many great ways to challenge your mind, such as:

- Do crossword puzzles.
- Play card games.
- Avoid playing the same games all the time.
- Play trivia games, which are easy to find online.
- Instead of writing a grocery list, create memory triggers for remembering what you need.
- Take a sentence from the newspaper and then try to make a new sentence using the same words.
- Try something, anything, new.
- Do jigsaw puzzles with children or friends.
- Listen to the news and then, later in the day, write down the main points.
- Drive home a different way from work.

Variety is the spice of life, but it is so much more. The key to avoiding mental sluggishness is avoiding monotony. People who lead monotonous lives are more likely to lose their "mental edge" and are unlikely to reach high levels of success. By experiencing new and different activities, you will develop a sharper mind, ready for new ideas.

Advanced Methods for Improving Your Mind

Yes, there is an art and a science to training a better brain. Your goal is to ramp up your brain's processing speed so you can read, organize, file, retrieve and act on information more quickly and efficiently. Brain training also improves your memory and learning capacity, as well as boosting your powers of attention, concentration and awareness.

The bottom line is that a speedier brain makes quicker and better decisions, solves more problems, and wins more games. While knowledge, wisdom, and experience are important, they lose their impact when names, words and ideas get stuck on the tip of your tongue, or lost in a mental fog.

If you really want to improve your mental abilities, MyBrainTrainer.com is like a gymnasium for your mind. You'll find lots of interactive activities that improve your ability to react with greater accuracy.

Baby Boomers Still Kicking

I'm proud to be a Baby Boomer. Our generation has been through a lot, and we're not going anywhere yet. We may not be as adaptable or knowledgeable when it comes to technology as our younger successors. But I want to tell you, if you are a Baby Boomer, you absolutely must adapt to today's technology. If you can learn about technology and the Internet, and apply your own life lessons and wisdom, then you will be more successful than any of your peers.

Aging does not put you at a disadvantage unless you allow your once sharp brain functions to dull over time. I still feel smart, attractive and happy. We older guys have wisdom that many young guys lack, but we must keep our minds sharp! I keep myself healthy and keep my mind sharp.

As I mentioned, the best way to keep your mind sharp is by trying new things. Let your brain know, "We're not done yet. It's only getting better." Whether it is starting up a new hobby, reading an interesting book or taking a different road on your way home, do something new and challenging. Are you stuck in a rut? Find a way out! Activate your brain again just by shaking things up.

The New System for Success:

- Your brainpower is just like your muscle power: use it or lose it.
- Try brain exercises to improve your time in The Thinking Room.
- Focus on improving all five senses: sight, smell, taste, touch, sound.
- Take on new, challenging activities to keep your mind in great shape.
- If you are a baby boomer, don't give up! Try new activities and learn new things.

Questions for The Thinking Room:

1. When is the last time you tried something new?

2. What is something new you can do today that will challenge your brain?

3. Do you feel discouraged by mental sluggishness as you age? What can you do to change that?

Chapter Eleven

Bowling Alleys, Classical Music and Baseball Stadiums

Have you ever been to a bowling alley? The noise can be deafening. There's no way a bowling alley is the best place to do your thinking. The very activity of bowling is noisy and destructive. Your entire goal is to throw one object, as fast as possible, hurtling towards other objects to knock them down. You would probably not choose a bowling alley as your ideal Thinking Room.

On the contrary, a room filled with classical music creates the opposite environment. The rhythm soothes, the sound of the orchestra invigorates, and the music has the proven ability to calm you and the surroundings.

Even if you've never considered yourself a classical music fan, the facts are undeniable. In 2004 the British

Transport Police piped classical music into London Underground stations in some of the area's most dangerous neighborhoods. After playing the music for six months robberies were cut by 33 percent, staff assaults decreased by 25 percent and vandalism went down 37 percent.

Some hospitals have also found that classical music increases the healing time of their patients. At the very least, it decreases patients' feelings of stress and anxiety.

Consider listening to classical music while you read the remainder of this book and notice the difference.

Where do you choose to spend your best thinking time? Are you selecting environments and activities that are chaotic and noisy or peaceful and invigorating?

Sometime ago, I went to a seminar where the speaker talked about how salespeople tend to have higher blood pressure and a higher pulse during a sale. If your pulse is skyrocketing and your palms are sweating, you really aren't able to do your best work.

To verify this for myself, I went out and bought a heart monitor. I discovered that my heart rate went way too high during ordinary conversations, and it increased even more dramatically when I engaged in tense conversations.

As I began to pay careful attention to my habits, I noticed that I spoke too loud and too fast. I noticed that I often felt hyper and anxious. I realized I had no habit of quietness.

Even though I've worked hard to improve my behavior, I still wear the heart monitor from time to time. It helps me understand what makes me anxious versus calm. The best thinking comes during the calm. That's why I recommend trying the heart monitor experiment for yourself. Use it as a means to read your anxiety level and begin to create more calm in your day-to-day interactions.

Find the Calm

Today's challenge is avoiding the noise and finding the quiet. We have so much noise in our lives, whether it's the soft whir of a fan, the sound of the phone, or the playful screaming and laughing of children.

How do you create a calmer space for yourself? Begin by turning down the noise.

People and situations in our lives can create metaphorical noise. For instance, people who always correct you, or those who constantly criticize, constitute noise in your life that you just don't need. You can turn down this "noise" by ridding yourself of unhealthy people and situations.

How often do you turn off your car radio? Just drive in silence once in a while. For me, I usually have music or talk radio on while I drive. But when I drive in silence, *wow,* the ideas really flow!

When do the best ideas pop into your head? For many of us, the greatest ideas come while we're waking up in the morning, somewhere between awake and sleeping. Or, if you are a night owl, perhaps these great ideas come to you as you are falling asleep. Either way, the fact that inspiration strikes in some of our most restful moments suggests that the best thinking is done in calm and quiet. Find the calm. Find the quiet.

My friend, Brian Decker, is a negotiator for the NFL. I asked him to tell me about Paul Tagliabue, former NFL commissioner. As a commissioner, Tagliabue did wonderful things for the NFL. I asked my friend Brian about Tagliabue's personality and mannerisms.

Brian told me that Paul Tagliabue had interesting behavior when in meetings. He becomes very quiet.

"What do you think he's doing?" I asked.

"He's thinking," Brian explained.

I'm so impressed that the best leadership can be done through quiet thinking. Do you know why? If others perceive you as a thinker, your value increases. If you think more and say less your peers, employees and family will really listen to what you say.

Better Breathing for Better Thinking

One of the most effective methods I've found for finding your calm place is focused breathing. You don't have to be into yoga to train yourself in breathing techniques. By simply taking slow, long, deep breaths, you will lower your heart rate and the symptoms of stress.

You can train yourself so that even under the most stressful situations, you feel calm and thoughtful. Think about how surgeons work. They operate for hours, focusing on intricate parts of the body and using small, specific tools. Someone's life is literally in their hands. They learn to breathe slow, mindful breaths. This keeps them calm so they can endure the stress of operating.

Professionals suggest that you inhale through your nose, counting to five and then exhale through your mouth, counting to ten.

We can all benefit from improved breathing techniques and finding the quiet. If you're still skeptical, consider these facts about the importance of oxygen:

- Oxygen is the most vital compound our bodies use.
- It is essential for the proper and efficient functioning of the brain, nerves, glands and other internal organs.
- We can survive without food for weeks and without water for days, but without oxygen we will die within a few minutes.
- If the brain does not get a proper supply of oxygen, it will cause degradation of all the vital organs.
- The brain requires more oxygen than any other organ. If it doesn't get enough, the result is <u>mental sluggishness, negative thoughts, depression</u> and, eventually, <u>vision and hearing declines</u>.

Based on this research, we can assume that oxygen is not just necessary for keeping our calm, is critical to our wellbeing. Consider practicing mindful breathing. Deep breathing from the diaphragm revolutionizes how you feel and how you perform.

The Quiet Mode

So maybe we don't always have access to a calm room playing classical music, with a gently bubbling fountain and a yoga guru chanting, "Breathe in. Breathe out." But here's the real secret: you can be in a quiet mode even when you are not in a quiet place.

A friend of mine manufactures baseball bats for the professionals. They are heavy! Sometimes I hold that bat and think about how the pros must feel as a ball is hurtling toward them at 90 miles an hour. If it were me up to bat, I'd be sweating with anxiety. I wouldn't know what to do. With thousands of screaming fans, bright lights and intense pressure, how could I function?

One professional baseball player told me that he doesn't hear anything when he's up to bat. He only sees the pitcher, the ball and his bat. He is calm yet focused.

If you can get into a calm mode, no matter how stressful the situation, you will achieve unbelievable success.

But by learning how to connect to our thoughts and how to find the calm, we accept our lack of control and find peace. We can overcome the negative thoughts that threaten our success.

My daughter Julie is a marriage and family counselor. After talking to her very first client on the phone, she called me in tears.

"My first client thinks I'm a salesperson. She doesn't think I'm a real counselor," she explained to me.

Julie was talking very fast. She seemed anxious. I had a feeling she had spoken to her client with the same rapid, stressed tone. I had a feeling she came off just a bit too frenzied. I suggested that she was probably nervous. I explained that in order to focus and command respect, she needed to find a quiet place in her life. From that place she could learn to speak to her clients in a calm, confident voice.

I recently asked her if she ever took that advice. She told me that finding that calm place within has proven instrumental in her career. She has found her own way to slow down and listen to the cues in her body.

Bowling Alleys Revisited

Ideally, your thinking room is your den, office, workout room or patio. It should be free of clutter and chaos. It should be quiet or filled with classical music.

No, the bowling alley will never be the best place to think. But with mental focus and breathing techniques, you can create a calm "Thinking Space" wherever you go.

Like the pro baseball player who doesn't hear the crowd, you can keep your eye on the ball.

Like Paul Taglibue, who sits quietly during noisy meetings, you can lead your team to greatness.

Like my daughter Julie, who makes time each day for quiet breathing, you can achieve success.

You can attain success and command respect by slowing down. Find your calm in The Thinking Room, and carry it with you wherever you go.

The New System for Success:
- Chaotic, loud and cluttered spaces are not the best Thinking Rooms.
- Consider adding classical music to your daily routine. It will soothe anxiety and stimulate creativity.
- Learn techniques for better breathing. This will improve your physical and mental health.
- Teach yourself to enter a "quiet mode" even when you are in a disruptive environment or situation.
- Think like a baseball player, by "turning off" the screaming fans (noise) around you and focusing on the task at hand.

Questions for the Thinking Room:

1. In what environment do you do your best thinking? How can you improve your Thinking Room?

2. Why do you think classical music has such a positive effect on the listener?

3. Does your heart rate increase while you are in pressured situations? How can you calm down?

4. Practice breathing slow, deep breaths. What effect does it have on your mind and body?

Chapter Twelve

Give 100%
(And a Little Bit More)

Are the successful born that way? Not Necessarily!

First of all, what is success? Each person must answer for themselves. I think success is peace of mind, personal freedom and having enough money to do the things I want to do and the ability to take care of my family. What does success mean to you? Does it mean fame, money, family, creativity, helping others? Or perhaps it's some combination of these things. The important concept is that you define what a successful existence means to you, and then go make it happen.

I believe that teachers have tremendous potential for personal and professional success. My mother was a school teacher and my son John is a school teacher. John is a success in my eyes for several reasons. He is happy and truly enjoys his life. He helps children become smarter and healthier. He encourages young people to think and develop self-confidence. It's not an easy job! But consider what a rich and successful life he's created for himself.

My friend Barbara is also dedicating her life to helping people. Barbara wants to be a doctor. I know that even if there wasn't that big payday ahead, she would still become a doctor. John and Barbara are very successful people because they think the right thoughts and make good choices. I respect that they have defined success for themselves, instead of allowing their family or their culture to define success for them.

But I'm not implying that you must live a life of ultimate sacrifice in order to consider yourself an accomplished person. I'm simply saying that *you* must create your own definition of success. Don't allow society, your parents, your employer, your background or your peers to determine your definition of success.

Spend time in The Thinking Room zeroing in on your own definition. Write several of these definitions down in your Thinking Room notebook. Then select the most accurate phrase and read it every day.

Get Honest with Yourself

When I'm in The Thinking Room, I ask myself, "Coach, are you giving 100% and a little bit more?" Most of the time the answer is *yes*. However, sometimes I disappoint myself. Sometimes I just coast. I don't get in the game. I give just a little less than I should, whether it's to my marriage, family, health, business, golf game, finances or community.

But that's where the questioning comes in. I have only been given one life to live and I want to give 100% and a little bit more. Many times I have fallen short, but the important thing is that I always keep this goal in mind as a benchmark for personal success.

Redirect your Emotions

If people would give a little more each day, *wow*, what a difference one person could make. Sometimes when I have a long day, combined with a long week of work, I just get tired. Everyone gets tired. We get bored. We get frustrated. We get worn down. We get confused. We get angry.

All of these feelings are normal, but negative. You have to push past these very normal emotions. Acknowledge them, try to understand where they're coming from, and then devise a plan to move gracefully past them.

Or, try to redirect some of your energy to helping someone else. Giving beyond yourself is one of the keys to happiness.

Try giving 100% and a little bit more to someone else this week. I bet your energy level will increase and you will ward off many negative emotions.

Winners Give More

Sometime my sales reps do not work hard enough or smart enough to be truly financially successful. It's disheartening to watch people struggle like this. I've learned that most folks talk a good game but are not willing to do the things that winners do. Winners practice. Winners always put in extra effort. Winners work hard, but more importantly they work *smart*.

I know it's not easy. Nothing worthwhile is easy. The best things in life take a lot of effort and hard work. Many are not willing to pay the price for true professional success.

Winners also take a leadership role in their own lives. For instance, I don't use words like *wish* and *hope* when I take on a task. I *expect* to complete the task and I *expect* the completed task will lead to an event. Then I *expect* that event will lead to a positive result.

What if you have a big project at work? Do you find yourself saying things like the following:

"I *hope* the boss likes it."

"I *wish* this project were easier."

If you think like this, then you aren't expecting to win. A winner is completely prepared and knows that he or she will complete the big project on time with a "wow" result.

Why am I so insistent that you think correctly? Because your thoughts lead to feelings, feelings lead to actions and the right actions lead to winning results. Stay with me here.

Everything begins with your right thoughts.

If you think like a winner, you will become a winner.

Expect to win.

Winning Takes Practice

If you were a professional athlete, how much time would you spend in practice? You would spend 90% of your career time in practice, wouldn't you?

We don't spend enough time in practice mode. We tend to spend our time doing the same things every day, but rarely practicing and improving the important skills. For example, when is the last time you *practiced* listening? It's harder than you might think. In order to become an excellent listener, you need to *exercise* your listening skills. Once you've become a great listener, you can move on to communicating, writing, negotiating, and public speaking.

I do not see people practice in business. I see people spending their time on just about everything else, from planning their vacation to scheming ways that they might do less but make more. Try to invest more to your career and see what happens.

Find the Hidden Excuse

So often I need to tell myself, "Do it now." I need to hear it again and again and again.

When it comes to accomplishing big things, there is often nothing more compelling than procrastination. We keep waiting for that perfect moment. But as we sit and wait, crafting all sorts of excuses for why "now isn't the right time," days, weeks and months slip by.

For so long I wanted to write this book, but I just kept putting it off. Every time I wanted to do something fun, I couldn't help but think about how I should be investing my time in this book. As the months stretched on, fun became … not so much fun.

When you have a nagging task, activities you normally enjoy bring on feelings of guilt. Avoid this by finding the hidden excuse. I had a whole host of excuses for putting off writing this book: I have no extra time, I've never written a book and I'm not a professional writer. My family, co-workers and clients kept encouraging me to sit down and do it. So I finally challenged all my excuses by seeking professional support, creating a strict timeline and just diving in.

From traveling around the country and teaching seminars for our sales reps, I learned that everyone has an excuse as to why they're not doing better in the bankcard business. We also have some extremely successful reps that make a great living using our marketing system. They don't make excuses. They use the tools at hand to get the job done. However, I get calls every day from reps that want to do better with their bankcard careers. Most of them have become bogged down with excuses for why they haven't been able to succeed.

My advice to everyone: *find your hidden excuse.*

A salesperson might fear rejection, hate cold calling or not be excited about their product. We all have excuses for why we dodge success, whether in finances, relationships or business. Whatever it is, your hidden excuse is holding you down like an anchor to a ship.

Spend some time considering your shortcomings. Find the source of your doubts and fears. Be honest with yourself about your hidden excuse. Only then can you start to find a way in which you can give 100% and a little bit more every day of your life.

The New System for Success:

- Success means something different to each individual. Don't allow anyone else to determine what success means to you.
- Get honest with yourself about your dedication to your job and family. Overcome negative emotions by renewing your dedication.
- Winners don't make excuses. Go into every task in your life with an expectation to win.
- Practice the tasks you don't like to do. Learn to improve yourself.
- Challenge your excuses by finding solutions and taking action.
- Find your hidden excuse.

Questions for The Thinking Room:

1. How do you define success?

2. In what areas of your life are you giving *100% and a little bit more*? In what areas of your life are you NOT giving *100% and a little bit more*?

3. What is your hidden excuse?

Chapter Thirteen

Permission to Be Extraordinary

America is full of examples of extraordinary people who came from ordinary backgrounds. These ordinary people became extraordinary because they were *thinkers and believers*.

Every time I feel "stuck," I return to the Thinking Room. Sometimes I'll turn to the inspirational stories of other successful men and women who came from ordinary backgrounds. Then I look within, determined to do the creative best with what I have.

What separates the ordinary individual from the extraordinary individual? I believe it all starts in the thought process. That is why I've designated a place just for reflection. That is why I've dedicated an entire book to the activity of thinking! I want others to know that success, no matter how distant it seems, is truly within reach. You simply must take those first tentative steps toward greatness.

Ordinary people **can** do extraordinary things. Just take a look at the following success stories.

Inspiration from Extraordinary Examples

Abraham Lincoln

Born in the backwoods of Kentucky, Abraham Lincoln worked hard country chores instead of going to school. In fact, he had less than one year of formal education in his entire life! But he loved to learn and enjoyed conversation. This helped him become an excellent lawyer and debater. During one of the most difficult periods in US history, the secession of the South and controversy over slavery, Lincoln kept his eye on the major goal of keeping a united nation with freedom for all. As the 16th president, Lincoln showed that one ordinary person can do extraordinary things.

Amelia Earhart

Daring to challenge the "boys club" of piloting, Amelia Earhart was the first woman to pilot a plane across the Atlantic and the first person to pilot solo from Honolulu to California. She grew up with a difficult family life, but when she saw an airplane for the first time at 10 years old, Earhart discovered her passion. In an era when women weren't considered capable of flying planes, she proved everyone wrong.

Mahatma Gandhi

Though he had attended law school, Mahatma Gandhi had difficulty succeeding as a lawyer. Most of his education was self-taught. Gandhi studied great teachers and writers (like Jesus, Tolstoy and Emerson) and he began to think that non-violent resistance could completely change a society. He found clever ways to undermine the British, who occupied India. He used creative, thoughtful methods to make powerful statements.

Walt Disney

As a farm boy from Missouri, young Walt Disney loved to draw. A natural entrepreneur, Disney sold his drawings to neighbors. He quit school at 16 and joined the Red Cross. Ever the nonconformist, he painted his ambulance with cartoon characters. Disney suffered many bad business deals in his early days, but never become discouraged. As his animated film company grew, Disney invested $17 million to build Disneyland, changing the nature of amusement parks forever. Though opening day was a complete disaster (wet pavement, too many people and wretched heat), Disney knew success was imminent.

Wayne Huizenga

A serious entrepreneur, Wayne Huizenga began his career with just one garbage truck in 1968. He aggressively purchased independent trash collectors, and by 1983 Waste Management, Inc. was the country's largest waste disposal company. Huizenga also started Blockbuster Video and AutoNation. He owns hotels and a luxury yacht that can be chartered for $400,000 a week. Today, Huizenga is most well known for owning professional sports teams in Florida, including the Miami Dolphins. Yet it all began with just one garbage truck!

Dr. C. Walton Lillehei

Not a household name like the others, you may not realize that Dr. C. Walton Lillehei is the "Father of Open-heart Surgery." Lillehei was an average student in his early years, yet he went on to earn five university degrees. He pioneered many aspects of heart surgery, including the pacemaker and artificial heart valves. Though he took many risks, and some surgeries didn't result as he had hoped, he kept persevering with new ideas for heart surgery. Many have a second chance at life because of Dr. Lillehi's perseverance.

Lessons from the Successful

If you're saying to yourself, "I have nothing in common with these extraordinary people," you're wrong. You just need to look a little closer. Most of these people came from humble beginnings. As I've studied the extraordinary people I've drawn connections between their lives and my own. With those parallels in mind, I look to them for inspiration.

Following are 5 steps to help *you* begin the move from ordinary to extraordinary.

1. Get to know yourself.

Self-analysis is not just for the therapist's couch! Being able to honestly assess your actions and motivations is a key to successful living.

While spending time in The Thinking Room, ask yourself the "why" questions. Why do I act the way I do in certain situations? Why have I chosen my current job, relationships, and hobbies? What do I consider my best and worst qualities, and why? Where do they stem from? Unless we're committed to counseling sessions, most of us never take time to ask or answer questions about our life choices and our very nature. It's time to start.

2. Realize that you are not alone.

Once you think you know a little bit more about yourself and your motivations, go online and find success stories related to areas in which you'd like to see yourself succeed. You will feel motivated to learn that people just like you achieved amazing things. You'll be surprised to discover their interesting roots and backgrounds.

Get to know others who have experienced the same things you've experienced. One of the most empowering gifts we can give ourselves is a support group of caring people.

Never feel embarrassed or ashamed of where you came from. Your experiences have made you who you are, but you are not the sum of your upbringing. You are a unique individual carving out your own path with the help of your resources, friends and family.

As Abraham Lincoln said, "You have to do your own growing no matter how tall your grandfather was."

3. Stop comparing yourself to everybody else.

Do you constantly compare yourself to others? Many of us fall into this trap, but it is usually an unproductive habit. The rare exception might be comparing yourself to someone you admire and attempting to cultivate similar qualities in your own life. But simply comparing for comparison's sake will lead you down a road of self-doubt and destruction.

You are 100% responsible for your own life. Your life is unique to you and your experiences, so don't apologize for what is out of your control.

Here's one way to look to your own abilities for strength and confidence. Consider the fact that many extraordinary people are very skilled at one thing. They've specialized and mastered a skill, trade or craft.

Find something you are good at, and then become great at it. Maybe you're a pretty good public speaker. Become an incredible speaker by working on that specific skill. Once you succeed at mastering something, it extends into every area of your life. When you become great at just one thing, all of a sudden your self-image changes.

And when your self-image changes, you're less likely to waste time comparing yourself to others. Instead, you're motivated to work on yourself!

Now you're finding success on your own terms.

4. Hit the refresh button.

I hear people say they are "burned out." There is no greater enemy to success than burnout. Hit the refresh button. Stop what you are doing! Stop!

I was coaching a businessman recently. This guy was completely exhausted. He had no motivation at work anymore. He had lost the desire to invent and be creative. He hadn't vacationed for seven years.

"You have got to stop," I told him. "You need to take a week or so off. You need a Think Week."

"I can't. I have too much to do," he told me.

"No, you don't have a choice. You have to re-energize," I pleaded.

"I can't, I just can't," he kept saying.

"Your business is going to end up in the tank if you don't recharge," I told him.

Whether or not he's receptive enough to take this advice could determine his future success. Our creativity, which is an essential activity in The Thinking Room, cannot function if all we do is task, task, task.

Yes, tasks are important to your business and your life. But creativity is equally important. Our creativity is often put on the back burner as we charge ahead with our to-do list.

If I'm doing the same thing every day, am I wearing out the strategies? Am I wearing out the goals?

Do something different. Sneak away for a movie once in a while. Sit on the beach and think. Take a vacation. Take a road trip. Do something different!

If you want to change your life; if you want to change the world; you have to switch up your routine. *Hit the refresh button.*

It's like the old saying, "If you always do what you always did, you'll always get what you always got."

We make ourselves unhappy because we get stuck on a treadmill. You have to expose yourself to "what could be." Ask yourself daily, *"What am I doing differently? What could I be doing differently?"*

5. Find a mentor.

Who out there is doing something similar to what you're doing but better? Most extraordinary people *want* to help others. Pick up the phone and just ask. It's hard to initiate, but think of how flattering it is to the person you are asking. And imagine the great insights you'll get from someone who is a master at their craft.

We all need someone who cheers us on and gives us honest feedback.

Who is that person for you? If you've never enjoyed the benefit of a mentor relationship, I *seriously* encourage you to do so. A mentor can provide the best leadership you've ever experienced. It's a wonderful opportunity to grow your knowledge base and create opportunities for future success.

Giving Yourself Permission

Are you holding yourself back? Let me tell you, success is possible for anyone who invests time in The Thinking Room. Some of us feel that we don't deserve success. Or perhaps we feel guilty about our success.

Give yourself permission to be successful! Give yourself permission to do something extraordinary. Write it down. I give myself permission to _____.

The New System for Success:
- Become inspired by studying others' successes.
- Believe that you can overcome challenges in your background to become an extraordinary person.
- Learn the habits of the very successful.
- When you feel burned out, hit the refresh button.
- Give yourself permission to be extraordinary.

Questions for The Thinking Room:

1. What successful person from history inspires you? What sort of background did he or she come from?

2. Do you compare yourself to your peers in a negative way? Why? How does this affect your life?

3. What do you need to give yourself permission to accomplish?

Chapter Fourteen

Complete Fitness

To make the most of your Thinking Room experience, total fitness is your goal. You must become physically, emotionally and mentally sound.

You might be wondering what your physical or emotional health has to do with your ability to run a business or succeed financially. Let's be clear: They are all interrelated. But what's most important to success is finding a *balance* among the three components. When you enter The Thinking Room, analyze your overall fitness. Is there any one area where you are severely lacking fitness? Is there any one area in which you are investing a disproportionate amount of time of energy?

I created The Thinking Room to encourage the right thoughts for physical, emotional and mental health. Take intentional steps to create total self-awareness. Then take intentional steps to turn that self-awareness into personal success.

Physical Health

Most of us, especially those of us in business, ignore this area. For many, a dedication to physical fitness is nonexistent. I'm telling you that you absolutely need a physical fitness routine. I've been trying to lose weight, and it's not easy. But I never give up. I show up at the gym almost every day, and I often do my best thinking on the treadmill. If you can commit to exercising just an hour a day (whether it's at the gym, walking in the park or laps in the pool) you will completely evolve your thinking.

Exercising is the best vitamin you can take. While you are stretching or strengthening a muscle, you are literally growing. The stresses of the world require that we burn energy and gain strength. The reason I place emphasis on this is because exercise actually makes thinking possible. It connects mind and body, it creates new synapses in the brain, and it teaches pacing.

You can do great thinking while working out. You aren't answering your cell phone or checking emails. You have time to work your body and think. And perhaps, you just might lose a couple pounds, add a few years to your life, and boost your self-confidence.

The benefits of regular exercise include, as suggested by the American Academy of Family Physicians:

- Reduces risk of heart disease, high blood pressure, osteoporosis, diabetes and obesity
- Reduces some of the effects of aging
- Contributes to mental well-being and helps treat depression and anxiety
- Increases energy and endurances
- Helps you sleep better
- Builds the immune system
- Helps maintain a healthy weight

And exercise isn't the only component to physical fitness. Don't forget about the importance of a full night's sleep. The 2002 National Sleep Foundation *Sleep in America* poll found that 74% of American adults are experiencing a sleeping problem a few nights a week or more, 39% get less than seven hours of sleep each weeknight, and more than one in three are so sleepy during the day that it interferes with daily activities.

When we don't get enough sleep, each part of our life suffers. Our jobs, relationships, productivity, health and safety (and that of those around us) are all put at risk.

If you know that your physical fitness needs an overhaul, talk to your doctor about exercise, diet and sleep.

141

Or, consider enlisting the help of a nutritionist or trainer. A thorough approach to achieving physical health would require an entirely new book, if not several volumes.

The point I'm trying to make here, is simply that if your physical fitness is sub par, so too will be your performance. If you feel like your physical fitness is suffering, please invest the time and energy in reclaiming your health.

Emotional Health

Do you stop and think about your relationships? You can be extraordinary through your relationships. Consider expanding your emotional boundaries.

The number one relationship is the one you have with yourself. Are you taking care of yourself emotionally? Do you speak to yourself in a negative tone? Or do you give yourself a pat on the back for a job well done?

Are your relationships with others healthy? First of all, give yourself permission to get rid of dysfunctional relationships. As an adult, you do not need dysfunctional relationships, nor do you need to put up with them. You can create an appropriate distance from those who treat you poorly.

Choose relationships that enrich you, rather than drag you down. Be selfish about who you spend time with. You have just one life to live, and there's no time or space for unhealthy people.

Are you investing time in the important relationships? What good is it to achieve phenomenal success but lack people to share it with? My wife, children and grandchildren are my absolute priority. Nothing motivates me toward success more than they do.

Another important aspect to emotional health is giving back to others. My son John is a teacher, baseball coach and head of the football program at an Oregon high school. John and I often talk about human behavior and the spirit of mankind.

One discussion led us to the topic of why some people do better than others, even though they may be equally skilled. We agreed that this edge could be brought about by a coach, teacher or mentor. Parents often instill an "I can do it" attitude in their children. But if not, an outside source of inspiration such as a teacher, coach, mentor or even a great boss may be necessary to help someone discover their inner strength.

John thinks that helping people believe in themselves is truly the best gift that one person can give to another. Helping someone learn confidence and the attitude that "I can do it" is why some people make it over others. Help someone do better, and you really wind up helping yourself. This is John Tunick's life work.

Your relationships either nourish you emotionally or drain you. Carefully selecting and growing relationships will help you become an emotionally healthy person.

Mental Health

Just as physical exercise maintains body tone, strength, and endurance, mental exercising has positive conditioning effects for people of all ages.

That's where The Thinking Room comes in. You have choices to make. Education helps, but you don't have to be a Harvard graduate to attain mental fitness! You do, however, need knowledge. But as we know from previous chapters, knowledge is easy to obtain.

Do you have to become knowledgeable at everything? No. Start by becoming an expert at just one thing. Then, when you know everything there is to know about that one thing, become an expert at another thing.

One study found that business owners who read seven business books a year made 230% more profit than those who only read four. I read nearly 20 books a year.

When you learn something new, it's a like a pat on the back. When you feel smart about something, don't you feel good about yourself?

I often remind myself that I don't know what I don't know. That means I have blind spots in my life. I want to discover these blind spots and learn how to minimize them.

By managing these blind spots, you become a stronger, more competent person.

A simple example of a blind spot could be a regulation that you're not familiar with, such as an employee law. We have blind spots because we don't have the proper resources, or the right mentors or experts guiding us. We have blind spots because we don't do the research.

Nobody can make an excuse for lack of knowledge today. Education and knowledge are available for all, whether it is through a college course, seminar, book, magazine or online resources. You deserve to feel smart, even if it is just in one specific subject.

Never feel discouraged about your knowledge. This is one area of life that we all have control of! No matter who you are, no matter how much money you have in the bank, no matter your SAT scores, <u>you can learn something new!</u>

Keep your brain active and healthy. I'm proud to be a baby-boomer and I won't let aging stop me from conquering anything I put my mind to. I exercise my brain by learning new things every day. When the Internet started growing, I didn't shy away like so many others in my generation. I learned more about computers, technology and the Internet, and now I am an expert at making money online.

Apply the same mental focus to your own life and you will reap excellent rewards.

Finding the Balance

Do you aim for total fitness? Or do you get carried away with one particular aspect of the overall picture? Do you find yourself avoiding exercise? Do you pretend that your emotional health and relationships are just fine, even when they are declining? Do you spend any time exercising your brain?

All three fitness components must be in balance. To be very strong in two areas but incredibly weak in one is worthless. Basically, balance comes down to priorities. I think a true balance of priorities begins with understanding that nothing in life or business is perfect. Do your best to achieve physical, emotional and mental health. Extend grace to yourself when you don't achieve perfect health, but just keep trying.

Euripides, the Greek playwright, said it best when he taught "The best and safest thing is to keep a **balance** in your life, acknowledge the great powers around us and in us. If you can do that, and live that way, you are really a wise man."

The New System for Success:

- Physical fitness provides you with better energy and overall feelings of health.

- Achieving emotional health means getting rid of unhealthy relationships, improving your life's most important relationships and giving back to others.

- The gas pedal that keeps you going is mental health. So it is imperative that you keep your mind sharp!

- Aim for a balance of all areas of your life.

Questions for The Thinking Room:

1. What is a physical health goal you have? How will you accomplish it?

2. How are your relationships? Are some changes in order?

3. Does your mind still feel sharp? How will you sharpen it?

4. Are you balanced? Which area do you invest too much/not enough time working on?

Chapter Fifteen

Finding your Pace

So many people tell me how their schedules are 100% full all day long. They are half-complaining and half-bragging about their constant *busy-ness*. They think busy-ness is the essential component to success.

But keeping yourself this busy leaves little time for the most important thing: Thinking.

The art of pacing begins when you create the "big picture" for your life. Is the "big picture" that you are a professional? Is the "big picture" that you are a stay-at-home mom? What is **your** big picture?

Take a piece of paper and draw out several boxes. Fill them in with the many tasks your life requires. Continue making boxes until you have put down on paper every task you can think of: Eating, exercise, vacation, work, cleaning, family, personal growth, hobbies. Use as much detail as you can muster. Then take all the activities in your life and rate each of them.

Number 1 is, of course, *thinking*.

Number 100 might be *smoking cigars*.

This is a regular activity for my Think Week. By ranking and filing my various activities, I am able to make better choices. Over the years I have learned that carefully evaluating my tasks paves the way for success.

Not only do I use this method for my own life, I insist that my consulting clients do the same. How many people actually stop and consider their priorities? Is it more important to go and shoot pool with buddies or stay home to help your kids with their homework? Is it more important to get to work 20 minutes early or get 20 more minutes of sleep? Either way, those 20 minutes can make a difference in your success.

This is the process of pacing and prioritizing. This is what very successful businesses do. This is what very successful individuals do.

Your Time is Like a Puzzle

Have you ever put together a puzzle? There's a specific methodology. You start with the corners and then the outside pieces. Then you group together colors and shapes. And everyone tries to force pieces together that clearly don't belong. It takes time. But eventually, you take all the little pieces and they begin to come together to create *the big picture*. To achieve the *big picture* in your life, you have to break everything down into *little pieces* and then put them back together in *the proper order*. If you leave any piece out, the big picture won't be complete.

Many people simply go too fast. They are breaking the speed limit of life. They miss so much, because they feel tremendous pressure to produce and perform. If you go too fast, you won't gain the maximum benefit from the life experiences that surround you. If you go too fast, you'll miss some important pieces in your puzzle.

Success lies in connecting the pieces. And if you're going 100 miles an hour, you're going to miss some pieces. If you get frustrated and start missing or losing pieces, you'll spend much longer working on your big picture.

A great puzzle strategy is to step back from the activity every once in a while to look at your progress. You take a few minutes to investigate some of the pieces you've had trouble with. Then you begin again, perhaps on the opposite side, and see if your fresh perspective helps with some of the trickier pieces.

Part of pacing is learning to slow down and do a little research. Take some time to investigate. I admit I had to learn pacing the hard way. I did not pace myself as a young person. Nobody said, "Ron, slow it down." When you take time out to research your project, you end up saving yourself time and frustration in the end. Remember, just because you're going really fast, doesn't mean you'll finish first. Slow it down! Take your time. Pace yourself.

Success Comes from Relationships;
Relationships Take Time

Here's what happens when you go too fast: You can't build relationships. Yes, you may have acquaintances, but they're often shallow. It takes time to build solid relationships.

And I'm not just talking about romantic relationships, familial relationships and friendships. I'm talking about business relationships too. Those may take even more time. And the best business is built on relationship. No man is an island. Without relationships, success is futile, if not impossible. So pace yourself and slowly build solid relationships that will stand the test of time.

If you fall down, those steadfast partners will be there to pick you. Why? You've invested in them and they've invested in you. Losers lose because they didn't spend time building relationships. Who picks them up? Who cheers them on? Losers don't pace themselves. Losers don't build relationships, which requires pacing.

"How can I help somebody do better in their life?" is the daily mantra of a winner. If you think about others, it slows down your pace. It takes you out of the center. If you're moving too fast, you don't have time for others. And they won't have time for you.

What Makes you so Busy Anyway?

Seriously, where does your time go? Have you ever tracked your time in the same way a dieter tracks their calories? Try carefully journaling where all of your time is spent. This is the first step towards better pacing and time-management.

Your greatest priorities should not take a backseat to the busyness of business. I realized years ago that the most important thing in my life is being a good father. Isolating this priority has made all the difference. I decided to slow down and keep my family number one. I don't know how I did it sometimes. In the early stages of starting my business, things were pretty crazy. But I chose to rate my family as the greatest priority.

And the best gift I've given myself is that I have no regrets. When I hear someone say, "I wish I would have spent more time with my family," I think about the pain he must feel to say such a thing.

He didn't pace himself. If you've lived a life of no regrets, you'll take your last breath knowing that you did it right. It doesn't get any better than that.

Don't allow yourself to fall into the trap of warp speed and instant gratification. Learn the art of pacing. Evaluate what you are doing and rate your priorities.

You have a long life to live. Pace yourself.

The New System for Success:
- List and rate all the activities and tasks your life requires.
- Think of your time management as a puzzle. Everything must be in its proper place for you to see the big picture.
- Don't allow yourself to become so busy that you ignore the importance of relationship building.
- Most of all: slow down and think!

Questions for The Thinking Room:

1. Which activities in your life are the most important?

2. If your time were a puzzle, would you say the big picture is emerging? Or are your pieces scattered all over the floor?

3. Think of a time when your busyness negatively affected your business or your family. What lessons can you learn from that experience?

Chapter Sixteen

When You Fall Down

You can fall down. You can fall down. You can fall down. And you can get back up, get back up and get back up. I've done it a hundred times in my life and so can you. All of us have moments of disappointment and dissatisfaction. In these moments of challenge, we are often immobilized by fear.

Why? Because we have not mentally prepared ourselves for such moments.

We haven't spent enough time in The Thinking Room considering the struggles we might encounter throughout the journey of life. The Thinking Room prepares you for life. This preparation will prevent fear from spoiling your most important moments.

The Greatest Applause

You can have tremendous success in this life not only in spite of, but perhaps because of your failures. Think about this. Sometimes the greatest applause is not for the winner, but for the one who tried the hardest.

Think about the races you've seen on TV or in person. Think about the person that fell down in the heat of the race but got back up and finished. And you thought to yourself, "Now, that's a winner."

So winning isn't really about coming in first place, is it? Winning is really about overcoming the fall and overcoming the temporary defeat. Winning is about pressing forward, even when you don't get exactly what you want, when you want it.

Winners Never Quit

When we don't get instant gratification, we tend to give up. And when we fail ourselves, we absolutely give up. The winning feeling is so fleeting, but knowing that you persevered stays with you for a lifetime. Every time you set your mind on a goal and work towards that goal, you will carry an internal confidence. And that leads to better results.

For thirty years I've worn a special ring on my right hand. The ring says, "Winners never quit." I grew up with a dysfunctional family, so I didn't understand the importance of perseverance as a child. I watched everyone around me give up. I never knew any different.

But through sports teams, and the help of my coaches, I learned that the real winning in life comes through the ability to keep going. It took me a long time to embrace the idea of *never giving up*. Every time I hit a bump in the road, I wanted to call the whole thing off. But then I learned the secret to winning: *just don't give up*. Keep going. Persevere. Never give up. And that's why I've worn this ring every day for thirty years.

Vince Lombardi said, "Once you learn to quit, it becomes a habit." If you quit even the smallest tasks, this psychology will penetrate into every corner of your life.

And it all comes back to thinking. If you are confronted with a challenge, whether major or minor, what do you do? Maybe you haven't been exposed to the right mentors. Maybe you haven't learned how to win. Maybe you haven't gotten good counseling. Well, guess what? You have one way to make up for it: challenge yourself to right the wrongs in The Thinking Room.

The Boogie Man for Grown-ups

Children around the world are scared that the Boogie Man may be lurking under their bed or in their closet. Well, adults have a Boogie Man too. We may act brave, but deep down all of us have fears that nearly paralyze us.

When we aren't prepared for life's struggles, including our own failures, we respond in fear. And as Franklin Delano Roosevelt said, "The only thing we have to fear is fear itself."

Why? Because fear immobilizes us. Fear paralyzes us. But fear can help us in its own way: it can send us into The Thinking Room. Though it's surely better to do all of the thinking before the fear strikes, if nothing else, fear motivates serious thinking.

You have The Thinking Room. You have a time and space designated solely for thinking. You can research the problem and think through the solutions. In fact, with the technology we are so fortunate to have, you can probably find someone else who has experienced the same challenge and has already paved the way for you!

That Good Ol' *Fight or Flight*

Even when you are in the grip of despair (and trust me, I've been there), your natural reaction is either fight or flight. Well, I'm telling you to do both at the same time. Take **flight** away from your problem by escaping to The Thinking Room. Then, **fight** the problem with your thoughts. Thinking is the best way to fight even your biggest problems. You win through your thoughts.

It's hard to consider *thinking* as equal to *fighting*. For many, just spending time in quiet contemplative thought brings to mind a hidden-away scholar or a meditative monk. But thinking isn't just for those with scholarly educations or the spiritually devout. Thinking is for each and every one of us. Each of us can become a scholar in our own way. *Become a scholar of what you need to know.*

Take fear head on and relish the idea that you have the right stuff to get where you want to go in life.

Everything Begins with a Thought

Winners know everything begins with a thought. And that thought leads to a choice: *I will* or *I will not quit.*

I recently won a huge local golf tournament. And I haven't won in a very long time. I was frustrated with my declining golf game, so I put some thought into it. I thought, "What is it about my golf game that is keeping me from winning?" I evaluated every club in my bag. I evaluated every move. I evaluated every thought I possessed toward golf. I spent time thinking about achieving a winning golf game. I realized my shortcomings (not getting the ball in the fairway and poor putting techniques). I improved on my shortcomings.

As I drove home from the tournament, I was pretty excited to tote that shiny gold trophy. Yes, it was a glorious win. But do you know what I'm most proud of? I never gave up. I knew I had "it" inside of me. All it took was some careful analysis of what I needed to change and improve.

But I'm not perfect. As much as I preach the power of thinking, I fall down all the time. I get tired. I get lazy. I get bored. There are certain problems that I just don't take to The Thinking Room, even though I know I should. I'm still learning, and I want you to join me.

Listen, everybody falls down. The only difference between a winner and a loser is that the winner gets back up. Losers say, "Everybody else is lucky." Or they say, "It's not worth it." They just give up. But winners tweak things and try again.

I'm not the first to make the metaphorical connection between life and sports, so I won't go too deep into it. But there's a clear connection between the two. In sports you win some and you lose some. The same is true for life. When you lose in life, just start preparing in new ways for the next game. Find the right coach and trainer. Practice your techniques. Prepare for winning.

You can fall down. You can fall down. You can fall down. And you can get back up, get back up and get back up. I assure you that applause will be even louder.

The New System for Success:

- Remember, the greatest applause may be for those who fall down and get back up.
- Dig deep within yourself to find your perseverance.
- Fear can paralyze you. You can fight your fears in The Thinking Room.
- Every action begins with a thought. If you think positive, you will lead a positive life.
- When you fall down, just get back up and keep going.

Questions for The Thinking Room:

1. Is there a time you quit and you now regret it?

2. Is there a time when you thought about quitting but instead persevered and now you are proud of yourself?

3. What fears keep you from persevering?

4. In what area of your life have you fallen down? How will you get back up?

Conclusion

Thinking Room Success

You entered The Thinking Room. You heard my story of hope and perseverance. You created an environment conducive to thinking. You took time out for a Think Week. You learned the importance of dating your decisions. You researched your fears. You became a scholar. You studied the successful thinkers. You never gave up.

I am proud of you and I hope you are proud of yourself.

My goal is that when you apply the concepts in this book, you will become a self-sustaining leader and a role model to yourself and those around you. This requires that you tap into a new system for success. It requires that you leverage the information of someone who had to learn many of his lessons the hard way. It requires you to minimize your own struggle by teaching yourself how to think.

I have shared with you the *New System for Success*. Many people will be surprised to find out that this "new system" is simply learning how to think. But it has to be right thinking. The New System for Success is **purposeful**, **planned** and **powerful** thinking.

Go into The Thinking Room with a **purpose**. You have to stop and take time to analyze all the things that are causing frustration in your life, your business, your finances and your relationships.

Time in The Thinking Room should be **planned**. Yes, there are opportunities to have spur-of-the-moment thinking sessions. But make sure you are also scheduling in time just for thinking.

Believe in yourself enough to engage in **powerful** thinking. As you build your experience bank, gain knowledge, and give yourself permission to be extraordinary, you will surprise yourself with the powerful thoughts that flourish in The Thinking Room.

Many people would see me sitting in my office, turned away from my desk, staring out the window, and think, "The President of this big company is just wasting time."

But that's where they're wrong. Time spent in The Thinking Room is the most productive element of my day. Instead of micro-managing my staff, I entrust them with details. Instead of spending twenty minutes picking up fancy, expensive coffee, I brew it here at the office and get down to the business of thinking. Instead of long, tedious meetings, I keep things brief and to-the-point. I prioritize and manage my time.

If you are truly seeking success then you will do the same. It will take some practice, but I have complete faith in your abilities. If you seek a balanced life of financial, emotional, relational, physical and mental health, then you absolutely must dedicate time to contemplation and analysis.

Thinking is never a waste of time. The time you spend in the Thinking Room is the best investment you'll ever make.

More Questions for
The Thinking Room

The first time you enter The Thinking Room can be a little intimidating. Perhaps it has been a very long time since you sat down with no intentions beyond thinking. Perhaps you are overwhelmed with the many tasks pleading for your attention. Perhaps you just don't know how to begin. In addition to the questions that followed each chapter in this book, here are more questions to prompt a stagnant Thinking Room sessions.

1. What can you do today to grow your income?

2. You are the product. A product developer is trying to improve the product. What changes should he make?

3. If you could have any job, any job at all in the world, what would it be?

4. What are your peers doing better than you?

5. What are you doing better than your peers?

6. What influence did your parents have on your attitudes (positive or negative)?

7. Who do you respect? What character traits do they have that you want to apply to your life?

8. When is the best time and place to do your thinking?

9. What relationships do you need to invest more time and energy?

10. Which is your favorite "hat" to wear? The business hat? The mom hat? The son hat? Which "hat" do you like to wear the least?

11. How have your fears defeated your efforts?

12. With what activity do you procrastinate most?

13. What is the biggest waste of your time?

14. Who is your biggest fan? What can you do to show
    gratitude toward that person?

15. Are you living your dream? Why or why not?

16. What task could you do today that would make you feel great?

17. What is the best lesson you ever learned from a boss?

18. What did this book teach you?

The Coach and You

Coach Ron Tunick is available for one-on-one consulting, group sessions, conferences and Thinking Room leadership summits. Using real-life examples and down-to-earth advice, the Coach keeps the crowd eager to learn. His unique, interactive Thinking Room session guides attendees through a process of better thinking.

For information on bringing the Coach to you, your business or your event, email coach@inthethinkingroom.com.

Additional books may be purchased online at www.inthethinkingroom.com.

I Want Your Stories!

Have you found success in The Thinking Room? How has The Thinking Room concept changed your life? Please email your testimonial to coach@inthethinkingroom.com and your name and story may be posted on the website or published in the next book.